my first origami book

my first origami book

35 fun papercrafting projects for children aged 7 years old +

Edited by Susan Akass

CICO kidz

Published in 2011 by CICO Kidz
An imprint of Ryland Peters & Small
519 Broadway, 5th Floor,
New York NY 10012
20–21 Jockey's Fields,
London WC1R 4BW

www.cicobooks.com

10 9 8 7 6 5 4 3 2 1

Text copyright © CICO Books 2011, plus
the project-makers listed on page 127
Design, photography, and illustration
copyright © CICO Books 2011

A CIP catalog record for this book is
available from the Library of Congress
and the British Library.

ISBN: 978-1-907563-70-6

Printed in China

Editor: Susan Akass
Designer: Elizabeth Healey
Illustration: Rachel Boulton, John
Woodcock, Hannah George, and
Stephen Dew
See page 127 for photography credits.

Contents

Introduction

Origami is almost like magic. You will amaze your friends as they watch you begin with a flat piece of paper and end up with a leaping frog, a glider, or an inflatable balloon—and all through folding. **My First Origami Book** will guide you through some of the simplest models, giving you full instructions and easy-to-follow pictures, and will gradually take you through to some trickier projects.

There are five chapters from which to choose ideas—Amazing Animals, Flying Fun, Top Toys, Dazzling Decorations, and Gorgeous Gifts and Cards. Plus, we haven't kept strictly to traditional origami. There are other paper-folding projects, too, some of which involve scissors and glue.

To help you get started, we have graded all the projects with one, two, or three smiley faces. The level one projects are the simplest. The folds are all very easy and there aren't too many stages. The level two projects need you to use some slightly trickier folds and are a little longer. The level three projects are for the expert folders who have begun to master more complicated moves, such as reverse folds, and who are happy to keep folding through many more stages to achieve truly magical results.

We have also included a techniques section (see page 116) to help you learn the techniques needed for each project. And if you're not sure what any of the arrows next to the artworks mean, check out the key on page 119.

Happy folding!

Project levels

Level 1
These use just a few folds and are very easy.

Level 2
These use more folds and are a little bit more difficult.

Level 3
These are longer projects with more complicated folding.

Materials you will need

At the beginning of each project, we have listed the materials you need—for most, no more than a piece of paper. You may want to buy one of the packs of special origami paper, which are available from craft shops, to make your models look even more professional, but you should also start collecting sheets of scrap paper to practice on and pretty wrapping paper for finished models. And for the papercrafting projects that move on from traditional origami, you should have a pair of scissors and some glue at the ready.

CHAPTER ONE
Amazing Animals

- -

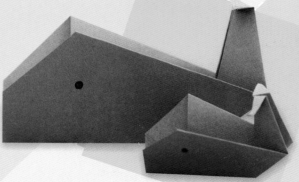

Fluttering **butterfly**

Find somewhere high from which to drop this butterfly and it will tumble and flutter to the ground. You can make it from beautiful patterned paper or decorate it with your own symmetrical butterfly designs.

A butterfly to flutter from **FLOWER TO FLOWER!**

1 Fold the paper in half from corner to corner and make a crease. Open it out and fold the other two corners together. Now you have a triangle with a crease down the center.

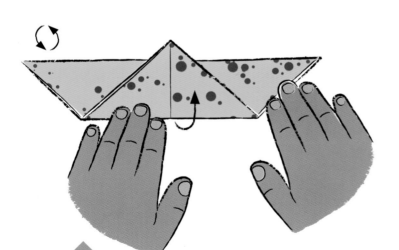

2 Have the point of the triangle pointing toward you. Fold the tip over so that it reaches about ⅜ in (1 cm) past the paper's edge.

3 Turn the paper so that the point is pointing left. Fold the paper in half along the middle crease. You now have a butterfly with its wings held up.

4

Fold down one wing about ½ in (1.5 cm) from the bottom crease. Turn the butterfly over and turn down the other wing to match.

Drop your butterfly and watch it flutter to the ground!

Wild whales

These fun whales are made using a very simple origami technique. You can make them in any size—how big will your whale be?

You will need

1 square sheet of blue or gray paper

Scissors

A black marker pen

1 Fold the paper from corner to corner to make a diagonal crease and open it out again.

2 Lay the paper flat on a table in a diamond shape, with one point toward you. Fold the two outer corners in so that two bottom edges of the diamond meet along the center crease. Press down the folds. You now have a kite shape. Fold over the top point of the paper to meet the top of the two other folds.

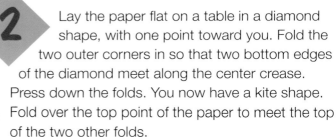

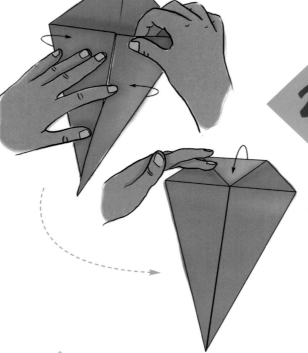

3 Now fold the whale in half along the center crease so that all the other folds you have made are on the inside of the paper. Press all the folded edges down firmly.

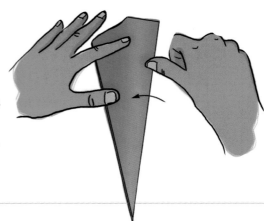

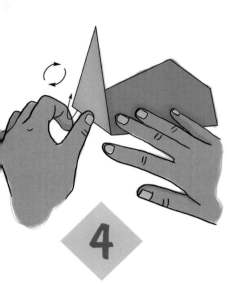

4

With the fold at the bottom, measure about a third of the way along from the pointed end of the whale's body. At this point, fold the tail upward at right angles to the body of the whale. Now fold the tail over to the other side to make a strong crease.

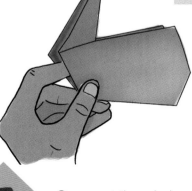

5 Open out the whale and push up the tail section inside the body.

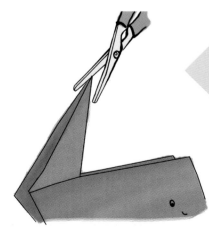

6 Use scissors to snip a ¾-in (2-cm) slit down the middle crease of the tail. Fold the ends outward to make the whale's flukes. Use a pen to draw eyes on the whale or stick on googly eyes.

Cheeky caterpillar

This jazzy little caterpillar is made from two lengths of paper that are folded together and finished with big googly eyes and cute caterpillar antennae.

A cheeky caterpillar with a **SMILEY FACE!**

1 Cut two strips of paper (one of each color) measuring 1 x 12 in (2.5 x 30 cm). Lay the two pieces of paper flat and at right angles to each other, with the ends overlapping. Glue the ends together, then press them down firmly. Let the glue dry.

2 When the glue is completely dry, fold the bottom piece of paper over the top one so that it lies flat at a right angle to the other. Do this again and keep folding until you have made the pleated body of the caterpillar.

3 Glue together the ends of the strips. Press them together firmly and let the glue dry completely. If you need to, trim off any overlapping paper from the ends of the strips so that the caterpillar's head is a square.

4 Stick the googly eyes to one end of the caterpillar and use a pen to draw on a nose and mouth. Snip off two pieces of pipe cleaner. Apply a dab of glue to the end of each piece and tuck them inside the layers of paper, just above the eyes.

Grazing cows

You will need two sheets of paper for this cow—one for the head and one for the body. You can color black or brown splodges all over one side of the paper as we've done here, but practice making your cow before you use your decorated paper. You will need to glue the head to the body at the end. Get skilled at this trickier project and you could have a whole herd of cows grazing on a green field.

You will need

2 sheets of paper,
6 in (15 cm) square

Paper glue

MOOOOOOOOO!

1 To start the body, fold the first sheet in half, then fold it in half again.

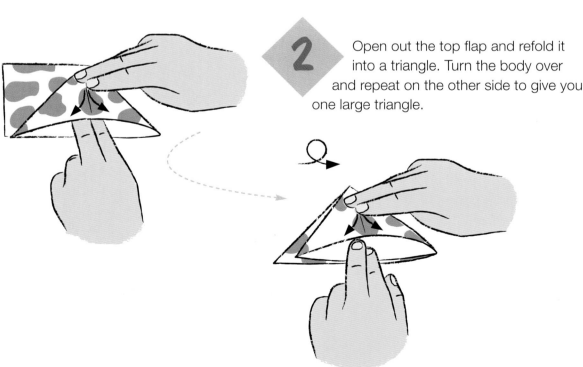

2 Open out the top flap and refold it into a triangle. Turn the body over and repeat on the other side to give you one large triangle.

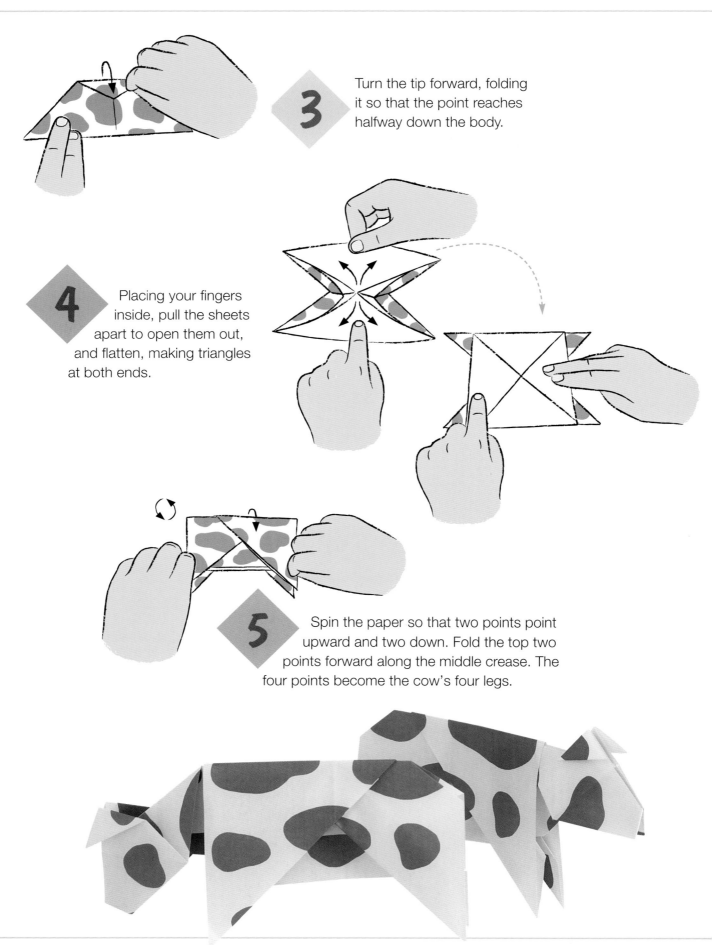

3 Turn the tip forward, folding it so that the point reaches halfway down the body.

4 Placing your fingers inside, pull the sheets apart to open them out, and flatten, making triangles at both ends.

5 Spin the paper so that two points point upward and two down. Fold the top two points forward along the middle crease. The four points become the cow's four legs.

6 Turn over one corner to make the rear of the body and fold it back inside, between the back legs.

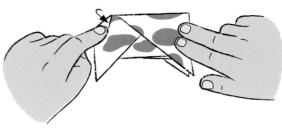

7 To make the head, fold the second sheet in half. Now turn the sheet 180°—so that the fold is at the top—and fold one edge up to the first fold line. Turn it over and fold the other edge up to the fold line.

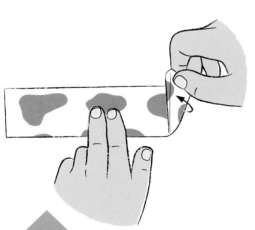

8 Fold the right-hand corner (all layers) up to the top edge to make a crease. Fold it back the other way to make a stronger crease.

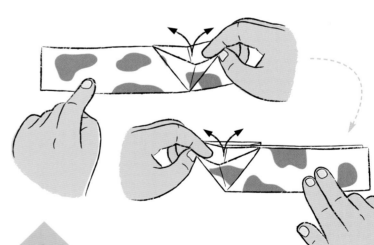

9 Unfold the crease, put your finger between the top two layers of paper, and open them out, pressing them down into a triangle. Turn the paper over and repeat on the other side. You will now be folding the left-hand side of the paper.

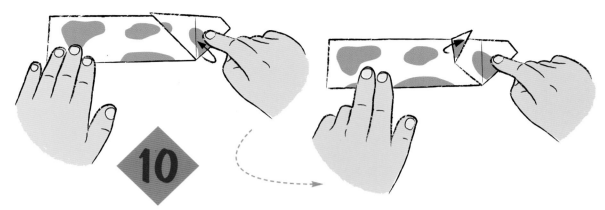

10 Turn the paper back over so that the triangle is on the right, and fold the end point underneath to make the nose. Next, fold the triangle's other point forward to make an ear. Make another ear in the same way on the other side.

11 Turn the nose inside out and press it back inside the head.

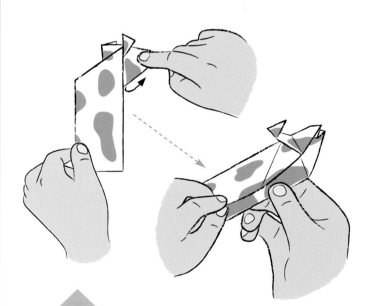

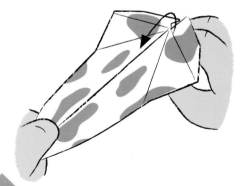

12 Pull the triangle that makes the front side of the head forward out of the way and fold the neck toward you at an angle, starting at the top of the head between the ears. The top of the paper will come to lie along the crease for the head. Sharpen this crease with your nails and then fold it back the other way to make a strong crease.

13 Open out the neck and then turn it inside out. (This is a bit tricky. Try holding the two halves of the nose together with your right hand and with your left hand hold the outside of the neck creases with your thumb and middle finger. Then push down the middle crease with your first finger.)

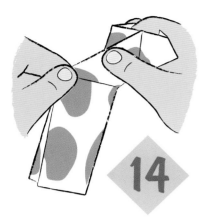

14

Run your nails along the neck crease to sharpen it again.

CREATE your own herd of PAPER COWS!

15 Turn over the bottom of the neck at an angle, then turn it inside out and press it back inside the neck.

16 Spread a little glue along the top of the neck and slide it into the body. Pinch the cow's back together for a little while until the glue dries.

Penguin pals

This design is easy to make, so you can create a whole family of penguins to play with. Obviously you will get the best effect if you use origami paper that is black on one side and white on the other. Make sure that you take care with your folds, so that your penguins stand up well.

You will need

1 sheet of paper, 6 in (15 cm) square

A line of penguins READY TO DIVE!

1 Fold the sheet of origami paper in half from corner to corner and make a crease. Open it out and fold up the bottom tip. Then fold the sheet in half again.

2 Turn back the top layer at an angle, then turn the penguin over and do the same on the other side.

3 Turn the long tip over at an angle across the straight edge to make the crease for the penguin's neck. Crease it to one side, then the other, and make the crease sharp.

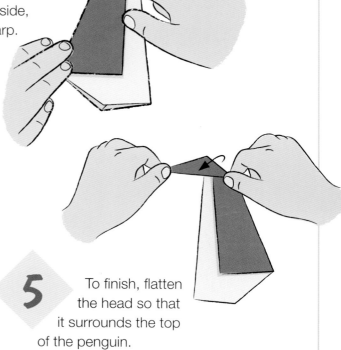

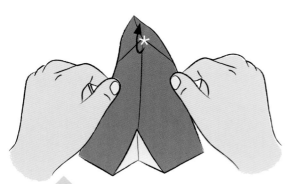

4 Open out the penguin and fold the tip back on itself to make the head, reversing the creases made in the previous step. It helps to push up underneath at point *, which becomes the top of the penguin's head. Don't turn the head over—it still faces in the same direction.

5 To finish, flatten the head so that it surrounds the top of the penguin.

Gorgeous goldfish

You could use orange and yellow paper for these beautiful little fish, or make them in white and decorate them. If you made a few special ones, you could hang them up to make a mobile for a newborn baby. The *kingyo* is one of origami's most magical designs from ancient times, as it is only in the last step it turns into a goldfish. This project is different from most origami projects, as you will need to make two snips with scissors.

Make a whole shoal of BEAUTIFUL FISH!

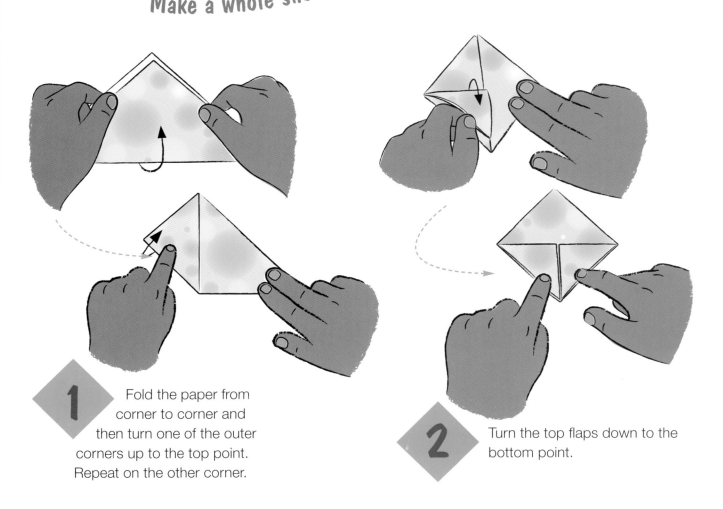

1 Fold the paper from corner to corner and then turn one of the outer corners up to the top point. Repeat on the other corner.

2 Turn the top flaps down to the bottom point.

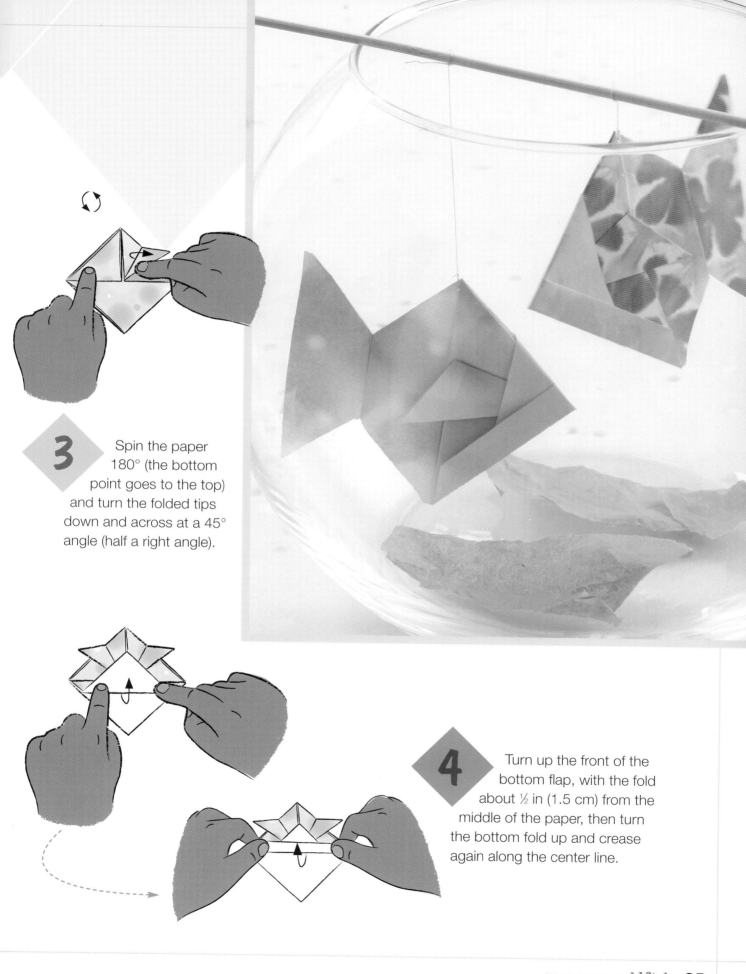

3 Spin the paper 180° (the bottom point goes to the top) and turn the folded tips down and across at a 45° angle (half a right angle).

4 Turn up the front of the bottom flap, with the fold about ½ in (1.5 cm) from the middle of the paper, then turn the bottom fold up and crease again along the center line.

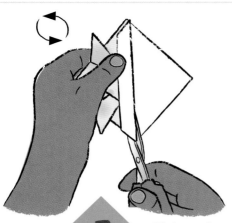

5 Pick up the paper, turn it 90° (what was the top now faces left) and use a small pair of scissors to cut ¾-in (2-cm) slits at the top and bottom, through the single layer of paper along the center line.

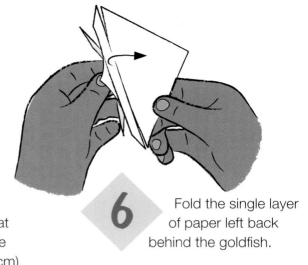

6 Fold the single layer of paper left back behind the goldfish.

7 Placing your fingers inside, pull open the object and flatten it down in the opposite direction.

How **FAR** will your fish **SWIM?**

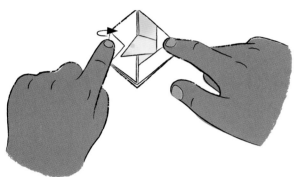

8 Turn over the left-hand point to make a ½-in (1.5-cm) wide flap.

9 Let go of the flap and open up the bottom of the goldfish. Fold the flap back on itself, into the middle of the goldfish.

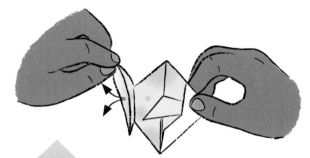

10 Pick up the goldfish and fold out the flap on the left to make the tail.

11 Flatten out the tail and your goldfish is ready to swim! You can draw on eyes and markings if you want, too.

Now make more fish to have a whole shoal of them!

gorgeous goldfish **27**

Freddie the hopping frog

● ○ ○

You will need

----

1 sheet of green paper,
6 in (15 cm) square

This little frog jumps when you push down on his back legs lightly with a finger. He is easy to make, so you and your friends can make one each and have competitions to see which frog jumps the highest. This is one of the most traditional origami models, dating from the days when there were not many toys for children to play with and they had to make their own amusements.

1 Fold the paper in half one way and then the other, so that it is creased into four squares.

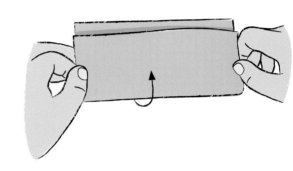

2 Next, fold all the corners in to the center.

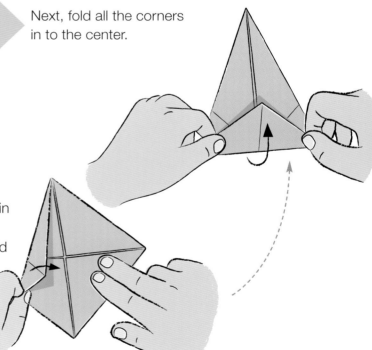

3 Spin the paper through 45°, turn in the outer points so that the edges run down the center line, and then fold up the bottom to make a triangle.

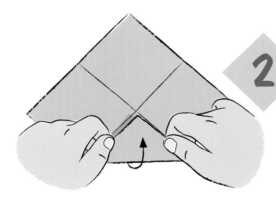

Have **FROG-HOPPING COMPETITIONS** with your friends!

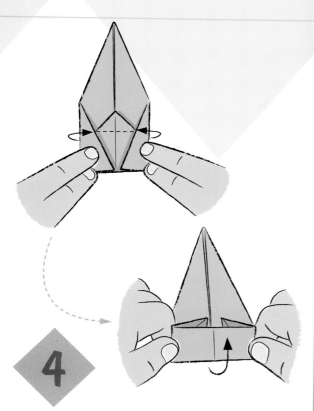

4

Turn in the bottom corners to the center line and fold the bottom up to the line where the corner flaps cross the lifted flap to make a crease.

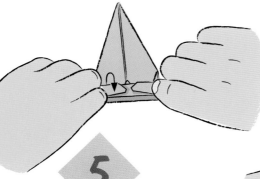

5

Fold the flap made in step 3 in half, bringing the end back down toward you. There are lots of layers of paper now, so it is quite difficult to fold.

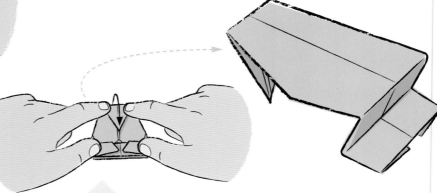

6

Fold the tip forward to make the head, then let the frog stand up. Push his back and watch him hop!

CHAPTER TWO

Flying Fun

Classic airplane

What do you do with a piece of scrap paper? Make it into a paper airplane! Children have been doing this for years, and this origami design is fool proof. It's up to you to find out just how far your plane will fly. You can make paper airplanes almost any size—just start with a square piece of paper.

You will need

----

1 square sheet of paper

1 Fold the paper in half and make a crease.

2 Open out the paper and fold the corners from one side in to the center line.

3 Fold one side in to the center again to form one wing. Repeat on the other side to make the second wing.

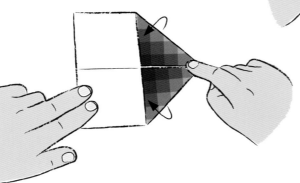

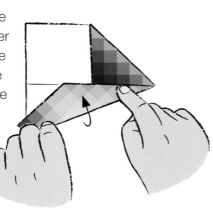

4 Fold back the tip by about 1 in (2.5 cm) to make the snub nose.

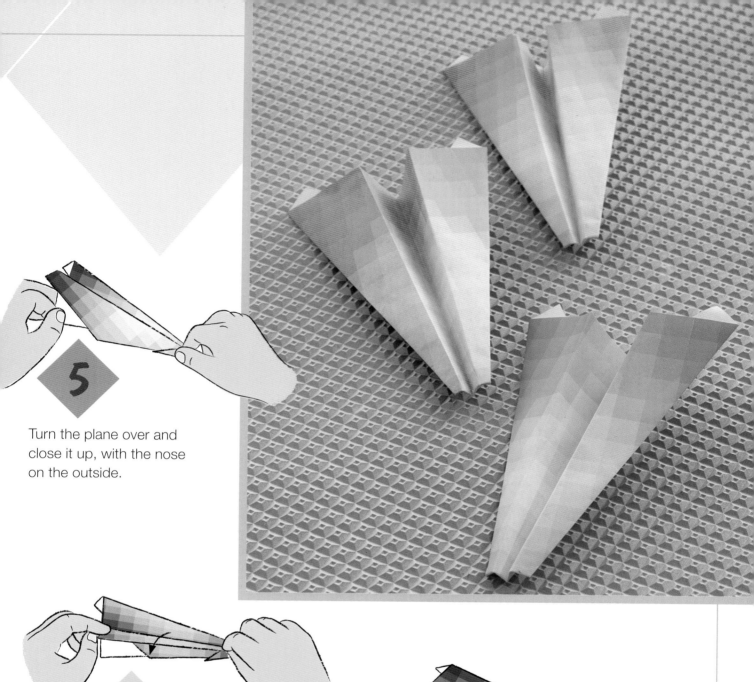

5

Turn the plane over and close it up, with the nose on the outside.

6

Fold down one wing and then the other. Make sure that the two wings are identical. You can experiment with different angles for the wing to see which flies furthest.

7

Open out your airplane and launch it!

Who can make a **RECORD-BREAKING** paper plane?

Long-distance glider

This simple glider is easy to make and it's a brilliant flyer. With a gentle throw, it will glide for miles. For technical experts, the trick is the double fold on the nose; it adds a bit of weight and helps the glider to go that extra bit further.

You will need

----

1 sheet of paper,
6 in (15 cm) square

Paper glue

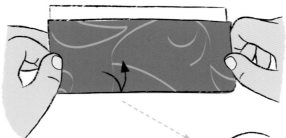

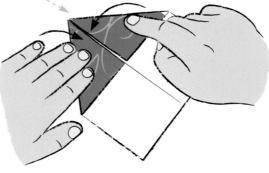

1 Fold the paper in half and make a crease. Open it out, then turn in the corners at one end so that they meet along the center crease.

2 Fold back the nose, making the crease so that the tip is about 1¼ in (3 cm) beyond the edges of the triangles. Then fold the tip back on itself, making the crease about ½ in (1.5 cm) from the first fold.

3 Turn the whole paper over and fold the glider in half along the central crease.

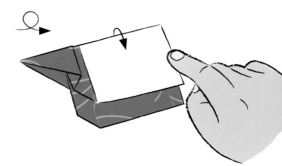

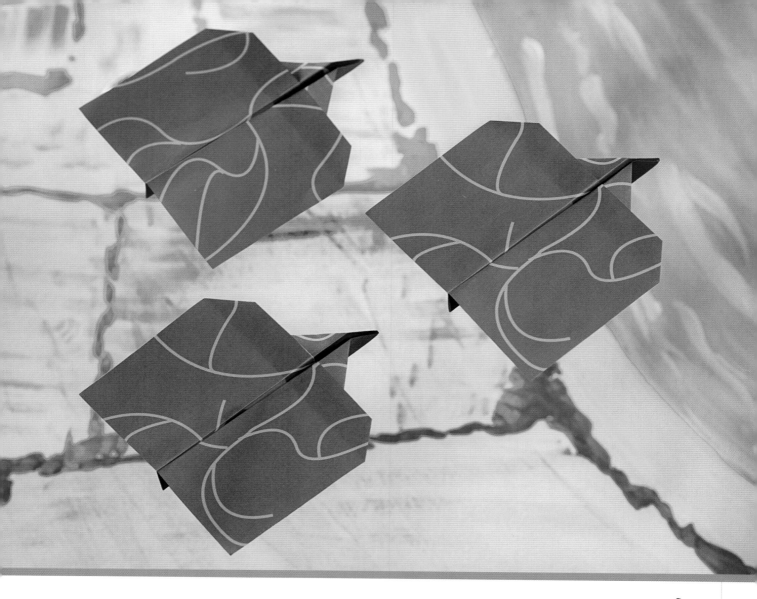

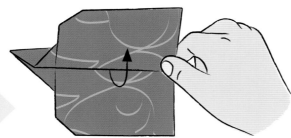

4

Turn back the top wing making the fold in line with, and about 1¼ in (3 cm) up from, the bottom of the glider. Turn the model over and repeat on the other side.

5 Add a line of glue inside the body of the glider and press the two halves together.

GLIDE for MILES!

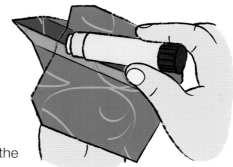

Jumbo jet

☺ ○ ○

The jumbo jet is yet another design of paper plane with which to impress your friends. While they are still playing with the basic airplane, you can be winning prizes with this different simple and effective model, which, like its namesake, can fly long distances.

You will need

- -

1 sheet of 5 x 8-in
(148 x 210-mm/A5) paper

1 Fold the paper in half widthwise and open out. Turn in the corners along one side, so that they meet on the central crease.

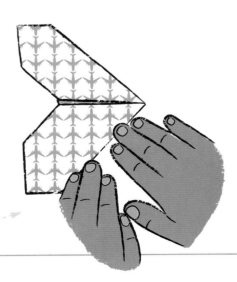

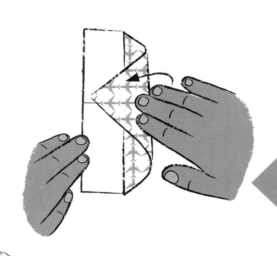

2 Next, turn the tip back so that it sits on the far edge of the paper.

3 Fold the far side across at an angle from the center mark, so that the front edge lies along the central crease, then repeat on the near side.

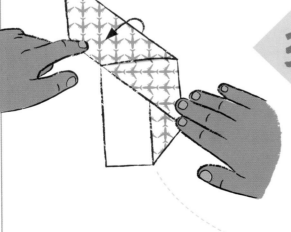

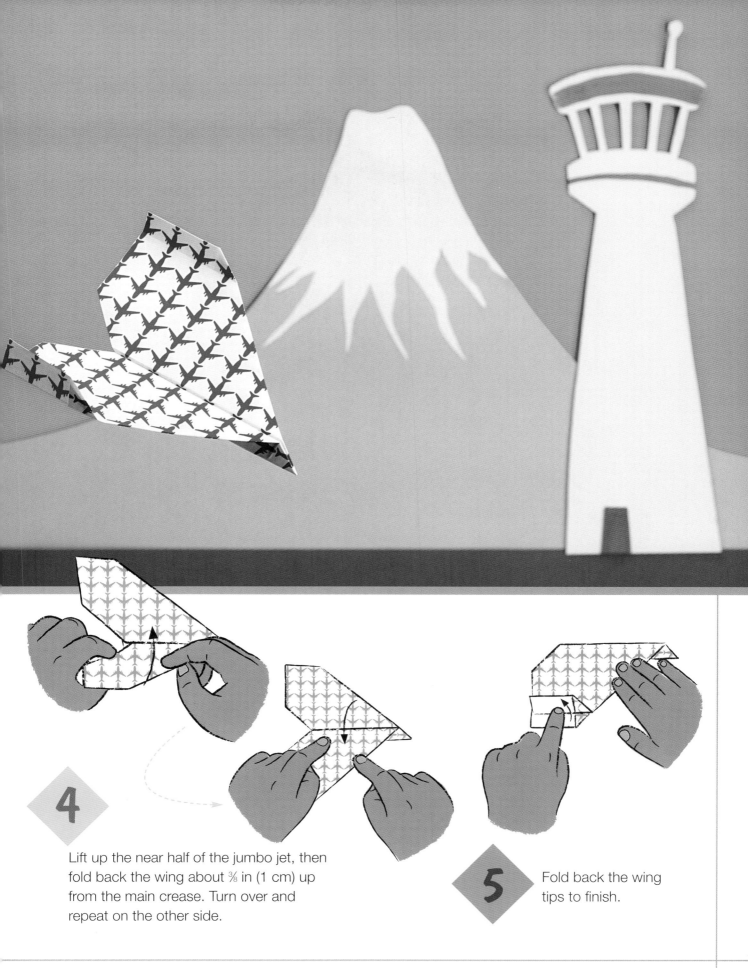

4

Lift up the near half of the jumbo jet, then fold back the wing about ⅜ in (1 cm) up from the main crease. Turn over and repeat on the other side.

5

Fold back the wing tips to finish.

Helicopter

The helicopter is a very satisfying model to make, as it is extremely easy to fold. When dropped from a height it rotates round and round, just like a helicopter, spinning evenly as floats toward the ground. Remember to take care with the creases so that the sides of the model match exactly.

You will need

1 sheet of paper, 6 in (15 cm) square

Scissors

Watch it SPIN!

1 Fold the sheet into three equal widths, then use the scissors to cut along the creases to give you three equal strips. These will make three helicopters.

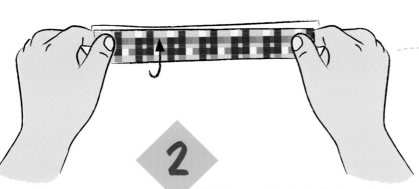

2 Fold one strip in half along its length to make a crease, then open it out. Make a second crease by folding it in half across its width.

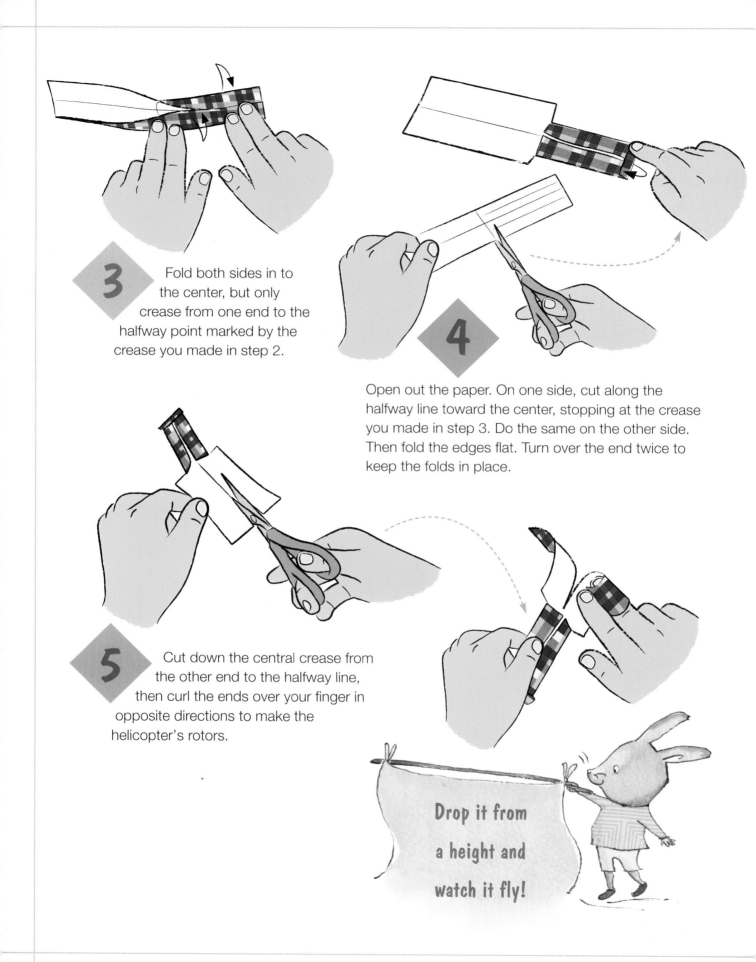

3 Fold both sides in to the center, but only crease from one end to the halfway point marked by the crease you made in step 2.

4 Open out the paper. On one side, cut along the halfway line toward the center, stopping at the crease you made in step 3. Do the same on the other side. Then fold the edges flat. Turn over the end twice to keep the folds in place.

5 Cut down the central crease from the other end to the halfway line, then curl the ends over your finger in opposite directions to make the helicopter's rotors.

Drop it from a height and watch it fly!

Heart kite

Why just send a card on Valentine's Day? This perfect little heart kite fluttering in the breeze will send your love in a much more original way. Decorate it with hearts or flowers and write your Valentine's message on the back.

Let's **GO FLY** a kite!

You will need
....

1 sheet of paper,
6 in (15 cm) square

Scissors

Sticky tape

Thread

A stapler

A drinking straw

12-in (30-cm) length of sparkling ribbon

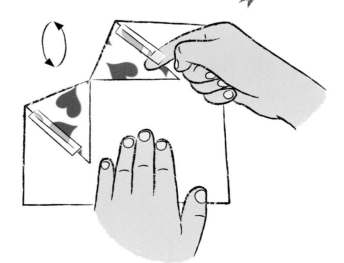

1 Fold the paper in half from corner to corner to make a crease, then open it out and cut along the crease for approximately 3 in (7.5 cm).

2 Turn back the two flaps at equal angles and stick them in place with sticky tape.

3 Fold the paper in half, then cut out the edge into the shape of half a heart. (Tip: practice this on some scrap paper until you have a good shape, then use it as a template to draw around.) Don't cut the flat fold at either side of the crease.

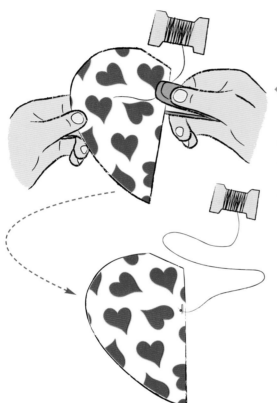

4 Attach a thread to the kite by stapling across it through both sides of the kite near the top, then fix the thread in place with a knot and cut off the loose end. The staple will hold the thread but will also keep a strong fold in the kite.

5 Open out the kite and staple one end of the straw to the widest part. Next, staple the other end of the straw to the other side of the kite. The kite should not be flat against the straw. Trim the straw to the right length.

6 Staple the end of the ribbon to the bottom of the kite, at the back. Then take it outside and watch it fly!

Magic ring

This magic ring doesn't look like a flying toy, but it's magic because it flies so well. You will need to master the knack but, once you do, your friends will be amazed by this fantastic flyer.

You will need

1 sheet of 5 x 8-in (148 x 210 mm/A5) paper

1 Find the center point by folding the paper in half—first lengthwise, then widthwise—and then opening it out.

2 Fold the paper diagonally through the center point so that the creases end up exactly on top of one another. This will mean that the sides are parallel.

3 Turn the paper so that the fold is at the bottom. Now turn the bottom edge up, using the outer points to show you where to make the fold. Now turn the bottom up again, halving the width of the flap you have just made. Next, turn over the whole bottom flap once more.

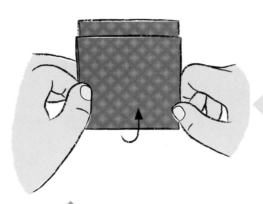

4

Curve the ring into a circle and join the ends together by tucking the right-hand side into the back of the left-hand side. Finish by tucking the loose end into the front.

5

Throw the ring by holding it from underneath with your middle finger and flicking it forward.

Flying brick

Make your friends laugh with this comedy airplane—it's even more of a joke if you decorate your paper to look like a brick wall! The brick appears to be too heavy and clumsy to stay in the air—but try making it and you'll find that it flies really well!

You will need

----

1 sheet of 5 x 8-in (148 x 210 mm/A5) paper

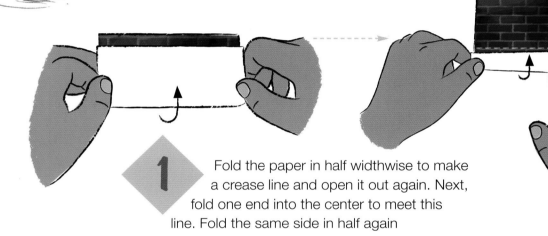

1 Fold the paper in half widthwise to make a crease line and open it out again. Next, fold one end into the center to meet this line. Fold the same side in half again

2 Fold the paper in half crosswise, but do not make a crease. Just press down the near point of the folded edge to mark the center and open out.

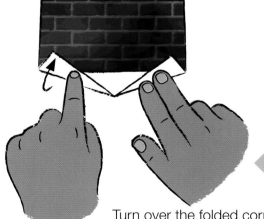

3 Turn over the folded corners, using the center mark made in step 2 as the fold point. Make sure that the sides match. You can experiment to see which angle of fold works best.

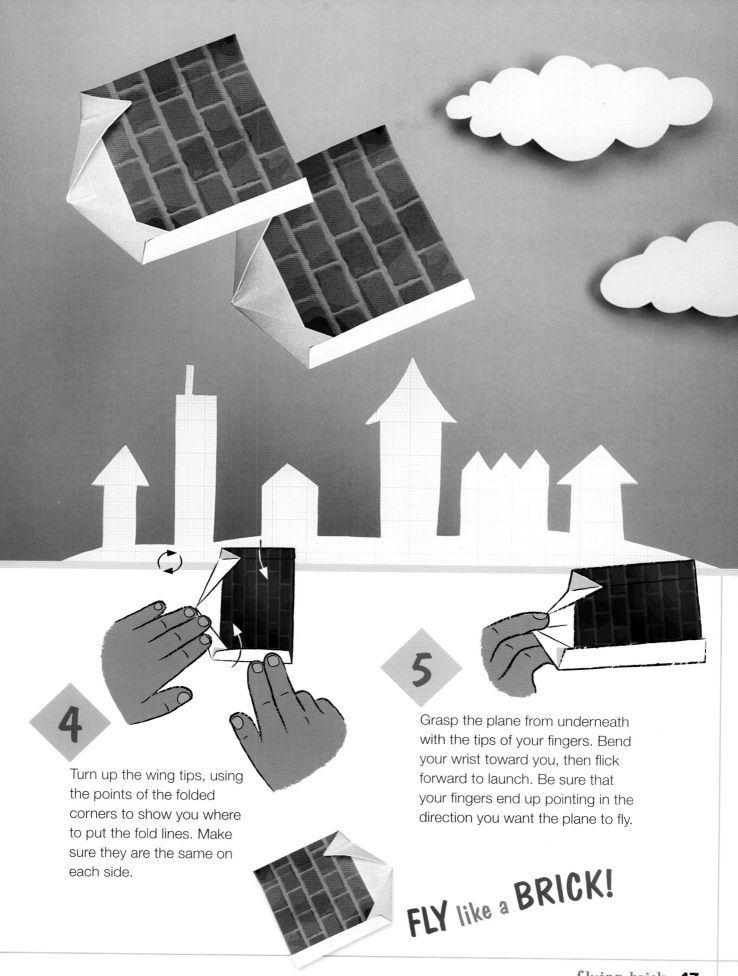

4

Turn up the wing tips, using the points of the folded corners to show you where to put the fold lines. Make sure they are the same on each side.

5

Grasp the plane from underneath with the tips of your fingers. Bend your wrist toward you, then flick forward to launch. Be sure that your fingers end up pointing in the direction you want the plane to fly.

FLY *like a* **BRICK!**

Top Toys

Party hat

● ○ ○

This hat is very simple to make and you can make it from any sort of paper, although stronger paper will make a stronger hat. Use colorful gift wrap, pieces of wallpaper, or even old newspaper. If everyone needs identical hats for a school play, here is the answer. If you need a hat for an Easter parade, make this one and decorate it with flowers, chicks, and eggs, or use Christmas wrapping for Christmas hats—the possibilities are endless.

You will need

1 square sheet of paper, 21½ x 21½ in (55 x 55 cm) for a child, 26 x 26 in (65 x 65 cm) for an adult

A hat of **MANY USES!**

1 Fold the paper in half to make a triangle. Bring the right corner across to the other side of the triangle, so that the top edge of the folded piece is horizontal.

2 Take the left corner across to match.

3 Fold the tip of the front flap down to the horizontal edge and make a crease. Fold the top edge of the same flap down to the horizontal edge and make another crease.

4 Open the flap right out again. You will have four equally spaced creases.

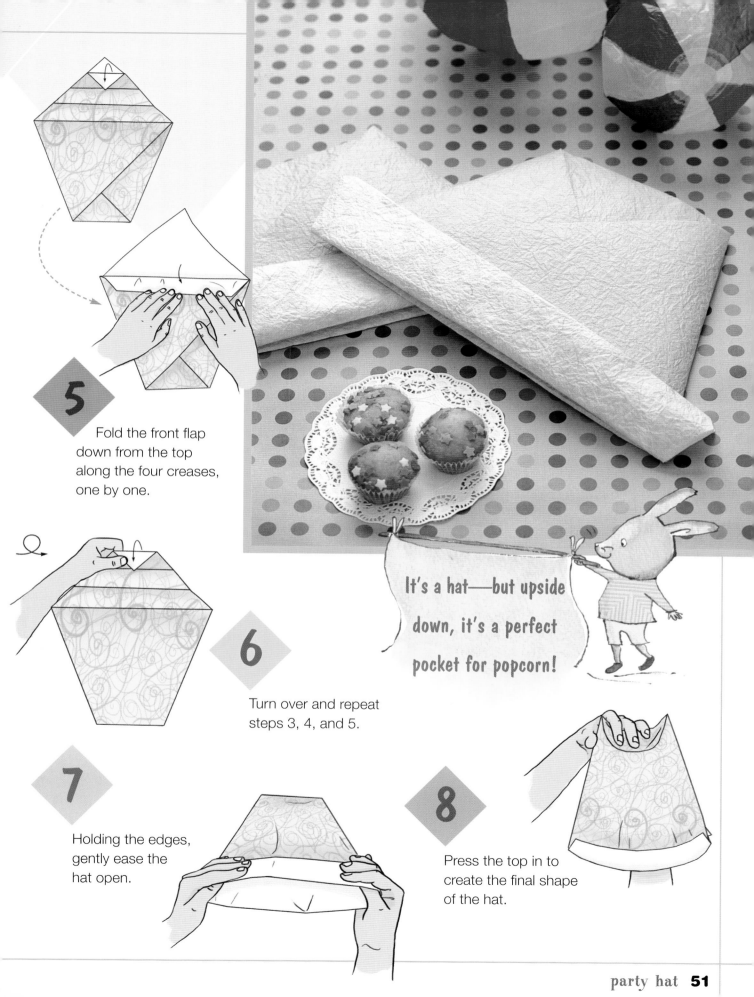

5

Fold the front flap down from the top along the four creases, one by one.

6

Turn over and repeat steps 3, 4, and 5.

7

Holding the edges, gently ease the hat open.

8

Press the top in to create the final shape of the hat.

It's a hat—but upside down, it's a perfect pocket for popcorn!

Color cube

Your teacher will really admire this perfect cube, which demonstrates all sorts of ideas that you will be learning in math over the years. But don't worry about the math. This is a really beautiful model, especially if you make it with six different-colored papers. It looks difficult, but is actually quite easy as you make the same simple shape six times and then slot the pieces together in a very satisfying way.

A MAGICAL BOX with no way in...

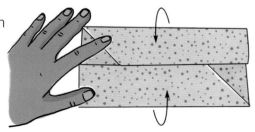

1 Take one sheet of paper and fold it in half to make a crease. Open it out and fold the top and bottom edges in to the center. Unfold them again and you will have three creases.

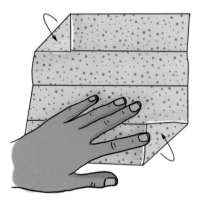

2 Lay your paper flat, with the creases running from side to side. Fold the top left-hand corner down to the top crease. Then fold the bottom right-hand corner (the opposite corner) up to the bottom crease.

3 Fold the top and bottom edges in to the middle.

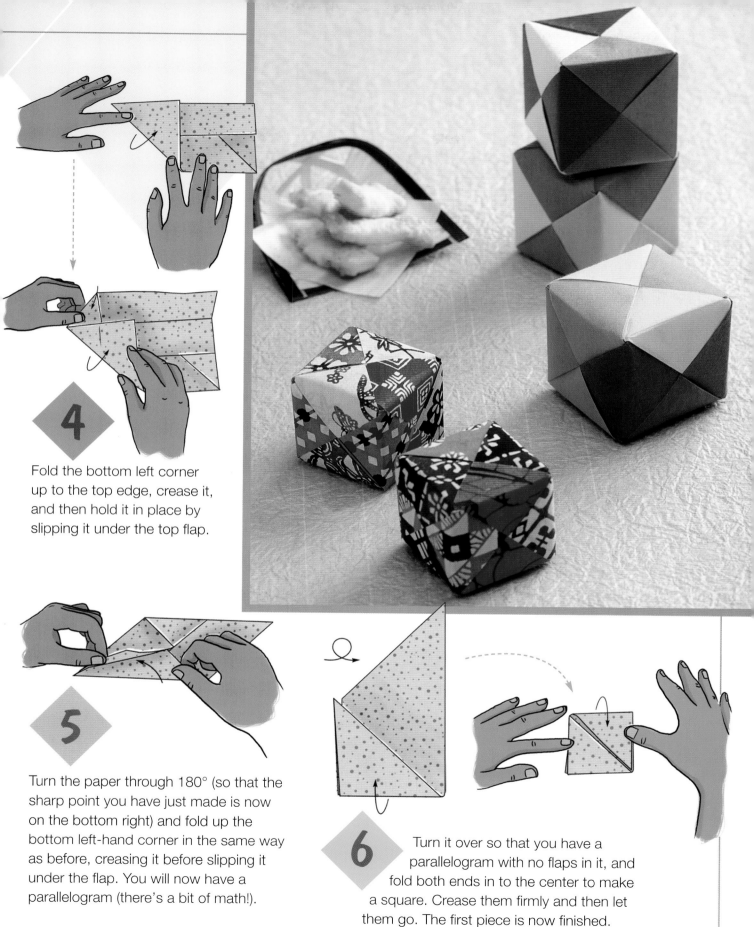

4

Fold the bottom left corner up to the top edge, crease it, and then hold it in place by slipping it under the top flap.

5

Turn the paper through 180° (so that the sharp point you have just made is now on the bottom right) and fold up the bottom left-hand corner in the same way as before, creasing it before slipping it under the flap. You will now have a parallelogram (there's a bit of math!).

6

Turn it over so that you have a parallelogram with no flaps in it, and fold both ends in to the center to make a square. Crease them firmly and then let them go. The first piece is now finished.

7 Make five more pieces in the same way, repeating steps 1 to 6. You will soon get very quick at it.

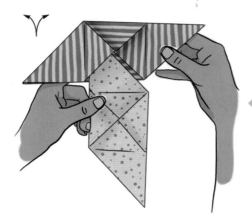

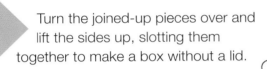

8 Slot four of the pieces around the first one by fitting the pointed ends into the slits in the squares, following the pattern shown in the picture.

9 Turn the joined-up pieces over and lift the sides up, slotting them together to make a box without a lid.

10 Fit the last piece in on the top as a lid, with the pointed ends slotting down into two outside faces of the box. The two last ends will still be pointing up. Fold these down and slot them into the top of the box.

11 This is a box with no way in. If you want to put a surprise inside, do it after step 9, before you put the top on. But whoever receives it will have to break open the beautiful box to find it!

Pacman the muncher

Handed down from mother to child, there are many traditional origami models and this is one of the simplest. Put your fingers into the holes, and open and close Pacman's mouth in every different direction. In England, this model is used as a fortune teller with colors and numbers to choose and a message to be found when you unfold it. Alternatively, place the Pacman upside down on a table to make a candy box filled with jelly beans for a party.

You will need
----
1 square sheet of paper

Pacman **THE MUNCHER** is ready to munch!

1 Fold the paper from corner to corner and make a crease. Then open the paper out and repeat in the other direction.

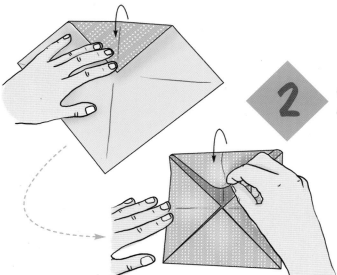

2 Open out and fold each of the corners in to the center.

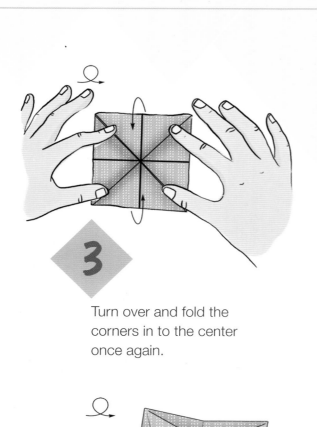

3

Turn over and fold the corners in to the center once again.

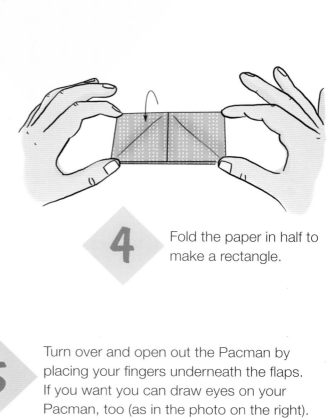

4

Fold the paper in half to make a rectangle.

5

Turn over and open out the Pacman by placing your fingers underneath the flaps. If you want you can draw eyes on your Pacman, too (as in the photo on the right).

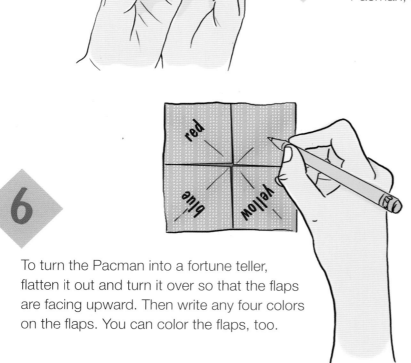

6

To turn the Pacman into a fortune teller, flatten it out and turn it over so that the flaps are facing upward. Then write any four colors on the flaps. You can color the flaps, too.

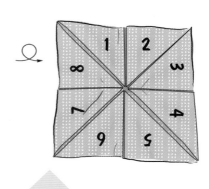

7

Flip it over and write eight numbers on the triangular flaps.

8

Open up the flaps and write eight different fortunes inside the flaps (underneath the numbers). Here are a few ideas you could use:

You will make a new friend today.

You will get full marks in a test.

You will meet your favorite singer.

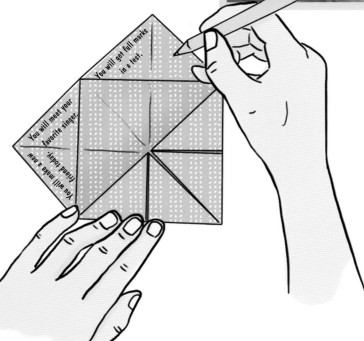

9 You can now be a fortune teller. Ask a friend to choose one of the four colors. Spell that color out, while moving the fortune teller in and out.

Then have your friend to choose one of the numbers that is showing. Move the fortune teller in and out the right number of times.

When you finish, ask your friend to choose one of the four numbers that are showing. Open up the flap they choose and read their fortune!

Blow-up balloon

This is one of the most magical of traditional origami models—one flat sheet of paper is folded in such a way that it can be blown up into a paper balloon. (Filled with water, it becomes a water bomb—but don't tell anyone...)

You will need
----
1 sheet of paper, 12 in (30 cm) square

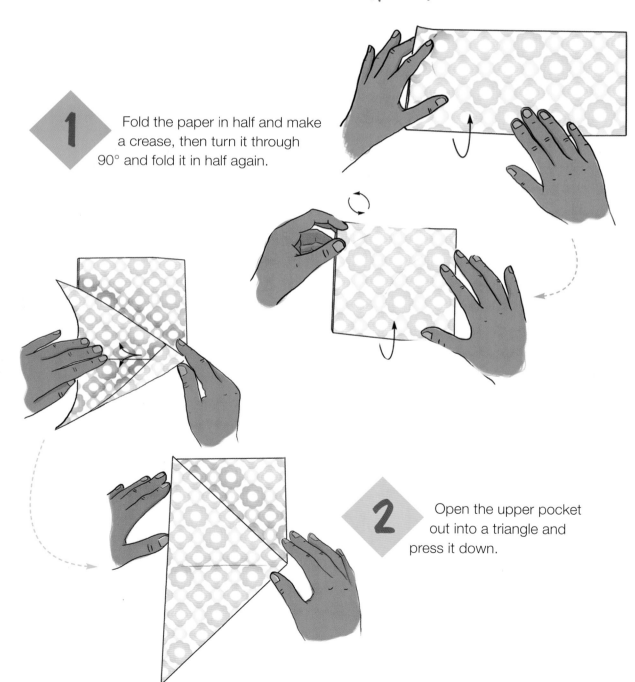

1 Fold the paper in half and make a crease, then turn it through 90° and fold it in half again.

2 Open the upper pocket out into a triangle and press it down.

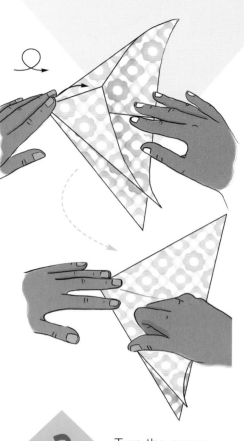

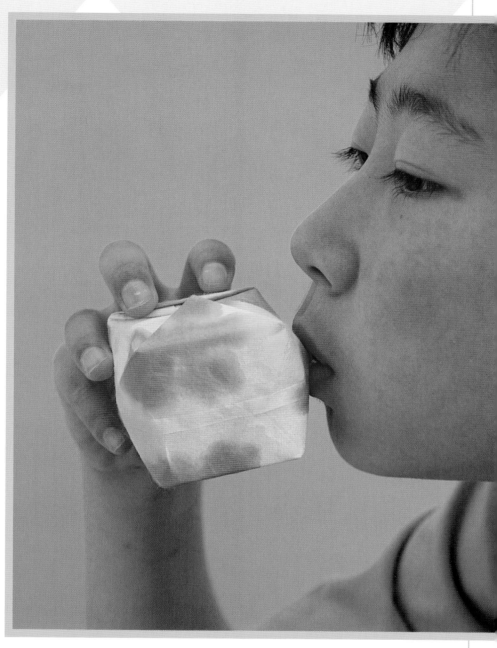

3 Turn the paper over and lift the square flap so that it can be opened out into a triangle, in the same way as in step 2.

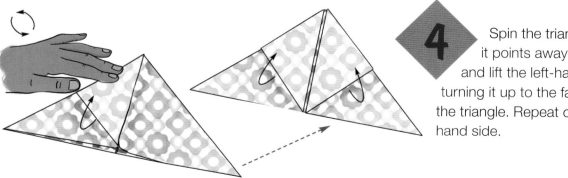

4 Spin the triangle so that it points away from you and lift the left-hand corner, turning it up to the far point of the triangle. Repeat on the right-hand side.

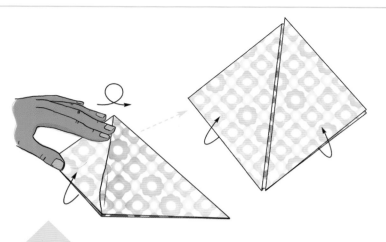

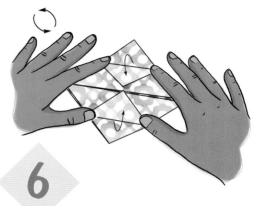

5 Turn the paper over and repeat step 4, making a diamond shape.

6 Spin the paper so that the slit in the middle runs from side to side, then fold the top and bottom points in to meet at the center.

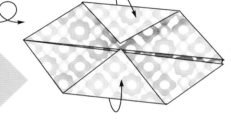

7 Turn the paper over and repeat on the other side.

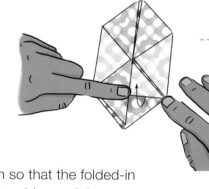

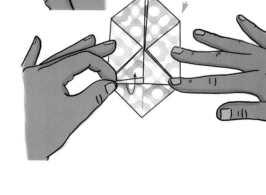

8 Turn the balloon so that the folded-in triangles are at the sides and there are two loose triangles at the bottom. Fold the lower tips of these loose triangles up toward the center to fit between the side triangles.

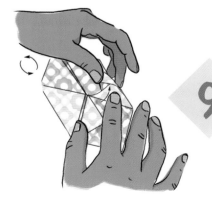

9 Now fold the two triangles you have just made across the two side triangles to make a crease and then tuck them inside the pockets in the side triangles.

10

Turn over and repeat on the other side.

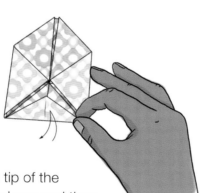

11 Fold the bottom tip of the balloon up toward you and then fold it back away from you, making a strong fold. Repeat with the top tip. Flatten the tips out again.

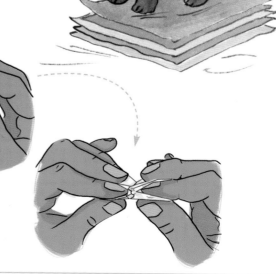

12 Open the sides of the balloon out into a cross shape and then blow gently through the hole in the top, blowing up the balloon while easing out the creases.

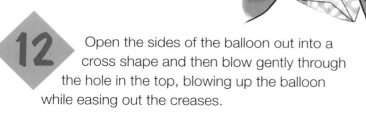

blow-up balloon **61**

Village house

You can make anything in origami: here, a simple house is created from a single sheet of paper. You could make houses in all colors and sizes and design windows and doors to decorate them.

You will need

1 sheet of paper,
6 in (15 cm) square

1 Fold the paper in half and make a crease. Open it back out, turn the paper over, and spin it 90° before folding it in half again across the original crease.

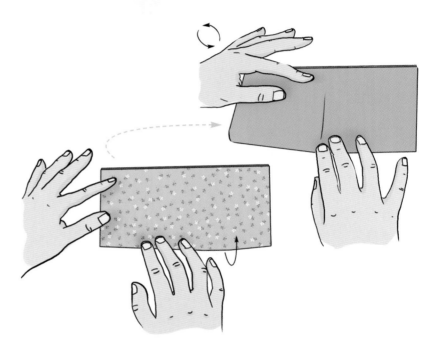

2 Fold the top part of the paper in half so that the edge runs along the center crease.

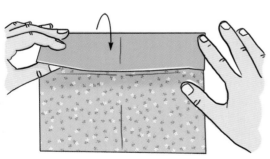

3 Turn the paper over, and then turn it through 90° so that the top fold is now on the right. Fold in the bottom edge to the center, followed by the top.

4 Turn the paper back through 90° so that the right flaps are at the top. Open out one of these flaps and fold it down into a triangle. Repeat on the other flap.

Make a VILLAGE OF ORIGAMI houses!

5 Make a firm crease by folding the bottom up to meet the triangle folds. Let it go to become the stand for the house.

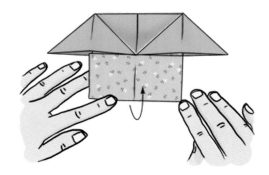

Samurai helmet

You will need

----

1 sheet of paper,
12 in (30 cm) square

A *kabuto* is a Japanese samurai helmet from the Middle Ages. Every year on Children's Day, Japanese people make this helmet to celebrate their children growing up strong and healthy. The helmet is often made from a sheet of newspaper for little children to wear, but you could also make it from colored paper as a party hat.

1 Fold the sheet from corner to corner to make a triangle, then bring one of the outer corners up to the top. Now bring the other corner up beside the first one to make a diamond.

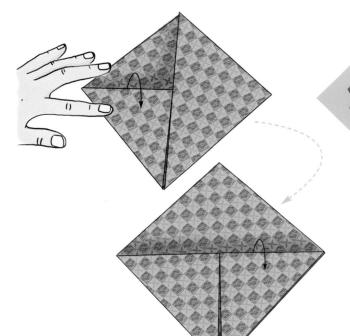

2 Fold the left-hand flap in half, bringing the tip down from the top to the bottom. Repeat on the right-hand side.

A **FEARSOME** Samurai helmet for your **TEDDY!**

3 Spin the paper through 180° so that the flaps are at the top. Imagine a line drawn across the middle of the right-hand triangle flap. Turn down the top of this flap so that its edge runs along the imaginary line. Repeat on the left-hand side. These make shapes like wings on the helmet.

4 Turn up the front triangle from the bottom so that the tip is in line with the top points of the "wings."

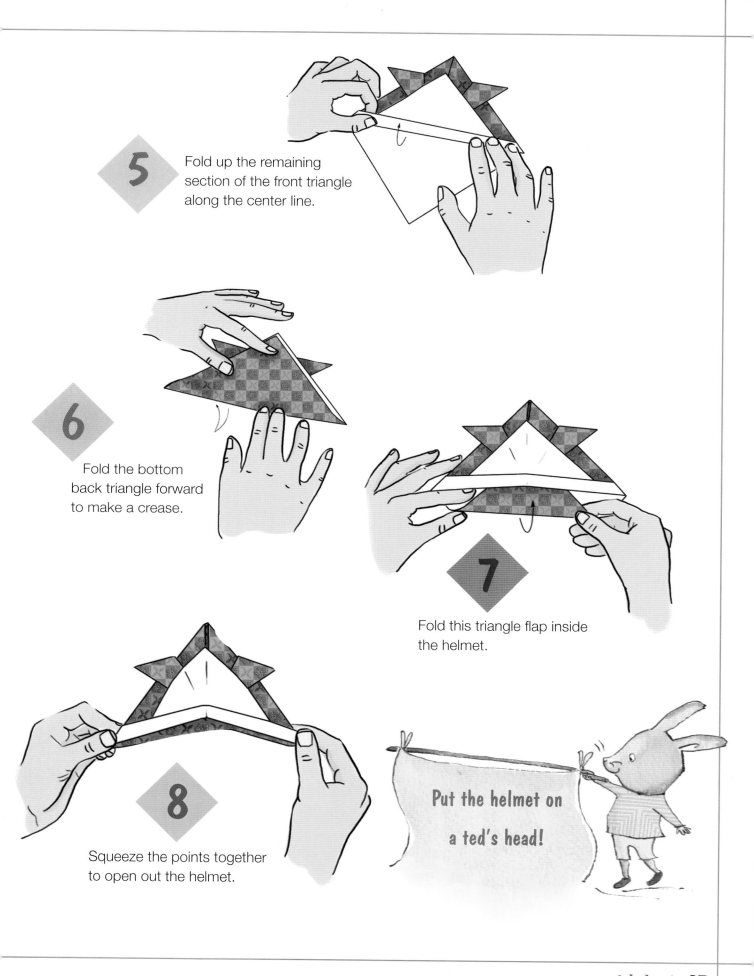

5 Fold up the remaining section of the front triangle along the center line.

6 Fold the bottom back triangle forward to make a crease.

7 Fold this triangle flap inside the helmet.

8 Squeeze the points together to open out the helmet.

Put the helmet on a ted's head!

Millefeuille cake

Millefeuille is a very popular cake throughout Japan, even though it comes from France where its name means "a thousand leaves." In Japan, there are specially printed origami papers for candies and cakes to make the models look almost real, but you can photocopy the template on page 123 or use it as a guide to color your own. Remember to practice making this slightly tricky model before you use any decorated paper. When you are good at making it, use the colored paper to make a paper cake that looks good enough to eat.

You will need

2 sheets of paper, 6 in (15 cm) square, for the cake

1 sheet of red paper, 3 in (7.5 cm) square, for the cherry

1 Fold one of the sheets of paper for the cake in half, make a crease in the middle, and open it out again. Fold the edges of the paper so that they meet along the center crease, making two more creases. Open it out again and fold it in half again along the center crease.

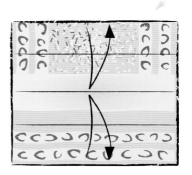

2 Fold the paper in half the other way to find the center—but don't crease it right across. Just make a tiny crease at one end with your finger and thumb. Now fold the sides of the sheet to meet at the center point you have marked, then open them out again to leave two creases.

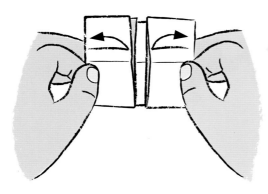

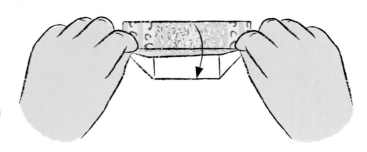

3

With the crease at the bottom, fold the bottom corners up at a 45° angle, then turn over the top flaps at the upper corners to meet the bottom corners along the center line.

4

Turn down the top flap, folding it along the central crease so that the top edge rests on the bottom of the paper.

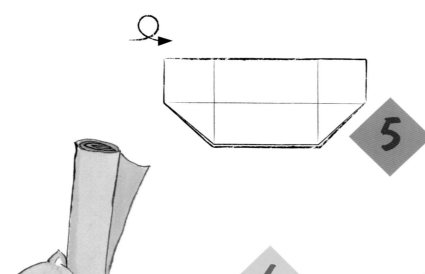

5

Turn the paper over—you will have a completely flat surface.

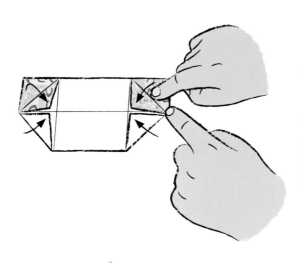

6

Fold down the top corners to the center line and then release them to leave diagonal creases.

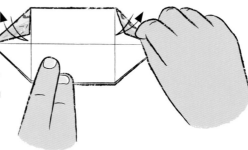

A paper cake that looks GOOD ENOUGH TO EAT!

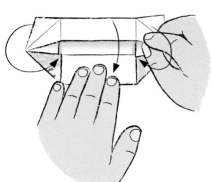

7 Fold forward the top half of the paper and tuck the triangle corners you have just folded between the two bottom layers. Flatten the paper out into a boat shape.

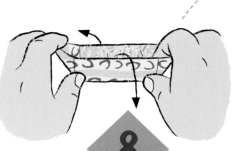

8 Lift it up and gently open the top of this "boat," pressing the ends straight. This will make a box with two sides missing.

9 Start at step 1 again, using the second piece of paper for the cake, to make the other half of the box. When you have finished, slot the two pieces together. (Note: the two tops overlap and the bottom is still open.)

10 To make the cherry, take the red paper and fold it from corner to corner and then in half.

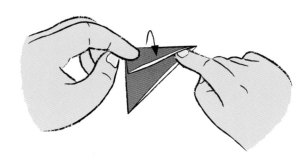

11 Lift one of the triangular flaps and fold it back as a square. Turn the paper over and repeat on the back.

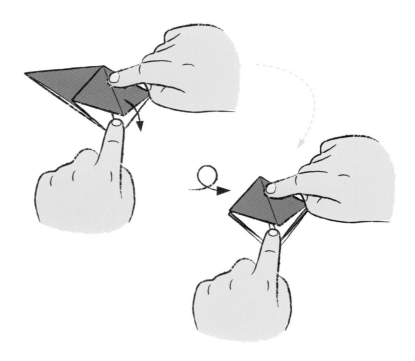

12 This bit is the trickiest. Pull up the top flap, push its side creases in to the center, and crease them the other way along the center line. This will give you a standing-up triangle. Flatten this triangle, pushing down its top edge to the center line. You will end up with a kite shape on top of a square.

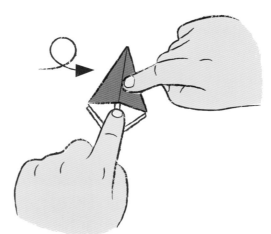

13 Turn the paper over and repeat on the back, lifting and refolding the top flap. Your paper will be kite shaped.

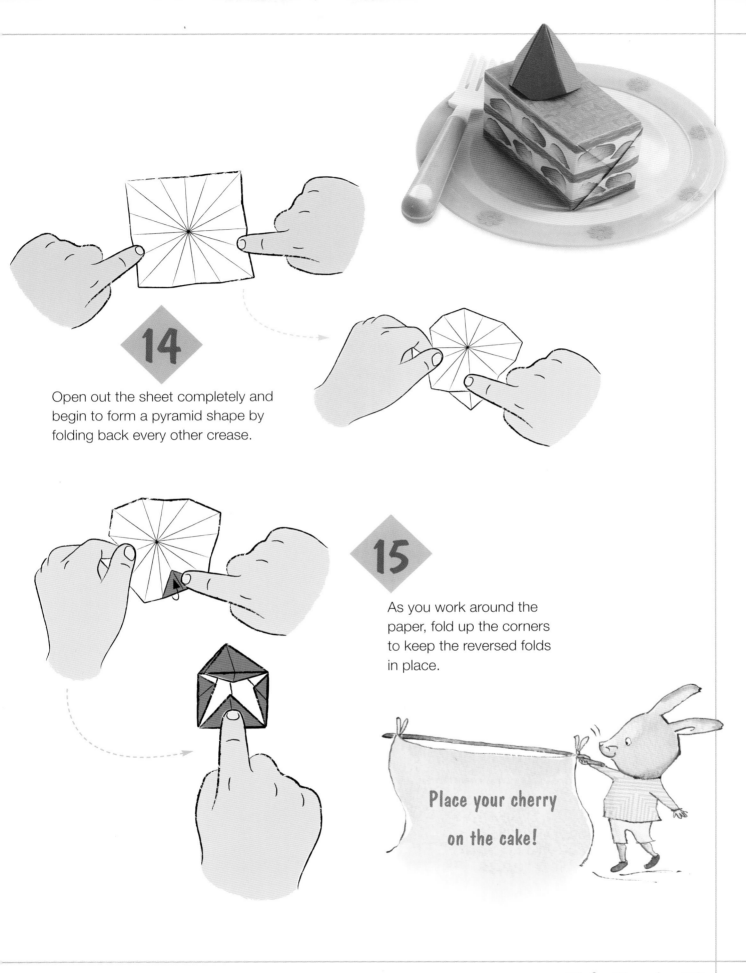

14

Open out the sheet completely and begin to form a pyramid shape by folding back every other crease.

15

As you work around the paper, fold up the corners to keep the reversed folds in place.

Place your cherry on the cake!

CHAPTER FOUR

Dazzling Decorations

- -

Paper bowls

Instead of sending paper off to be recycled, why not recycle it yourself into a beautiful little bowl? Use any paper, but the more colored paper you can include, the more interesting your bowl will be. You can use old letters, printed documents, circulars, and magazines that you would normally dump in the paper recycling bin. These bowls aren't difficult to make, but they are a bit fiddly—so the more patient you are, the bigger the bowl you can make.

RECYCLE paper into beautiful bowls!

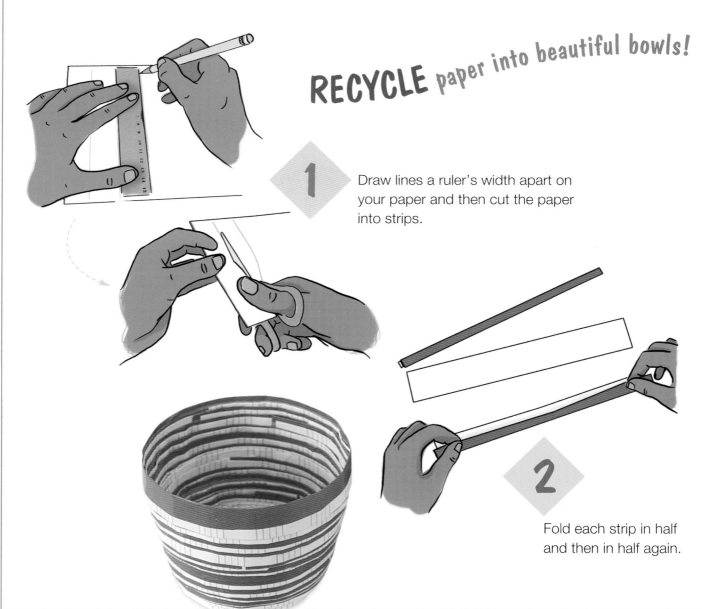

1 Draw lines a ruler's width apart on your paper and then cut the paper into strips.

2 Fold each strip in half and then in half again.

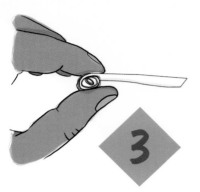

3

Start winding one of the folded strips tightly to make a flat coil, adding some dabs of glue to secure it as you go. When you have finished one strip, carry on with the next, adding a dab of glue to fasten the ends.

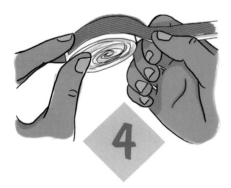

4

When the base is wide enough, begin winding up the sides. As you wind, place the new strip about halfway up the last strip, so that the sides begin to get higher.

5

Carry on winding, adding dabs of glue as you go, until the sides of the bowl are high enough. Add a final dab of glue to secure the ends.

Bird boxes

These attractive little boxes would make a great birthday present for your mother or grandmother. Look out for pieces of pretty wrapping paper or old wallpaper, which will make the box and the bird really colorful. If you want to be even more creative, design your own bird and paint or color it yourself.

You will need

A pencil

A ruler

11 x 17 in (297 x 240 mm/A3) thin white photocopy card

Scissors

Sharp-pointed scissors

Sheets of patterned paper in at least three different designs

A glue stick

A file paper hole punch (a one-hole punch is easier but you can use a two-hole punch)

1 Ask an adult to photocopy the templates on pages 124–125 using the 200% zoom button on the photocopier to make them double size. Make two copies directly onto white card.

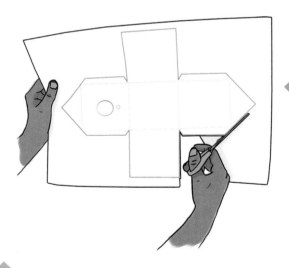

2 Cut out one bird box carefully, being extra careful not to cut off the flaps from the house template.

3 Use the second bird box copy as a pattern to cut the colored paper for the sides of the birdhouse. (Note: you won't need the bird and roof pieces on this second photocopy.) First, cut around the bird box carefully —but this time, you must cut off the flaps. Cut each side off the base. Use each side as a template to draw around, drawing on the back of the colored papers you have chosen for the sides. Cut these sides out carefully.

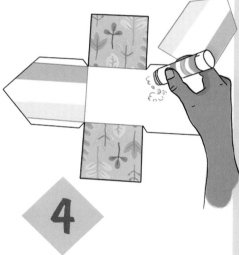

4

Place the white card with dotted lines face down. Glue the pieces of colored paper in place on the all-white side. Leave the glue to dry completely.

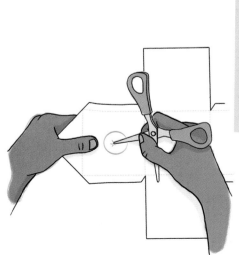

5

Turn the card over and, using the point of a pair of sharp-pointed scissors, carefully make a hole through the large circle shown on the template. Now cut neatly around the edge of the circle to make the bird's entrance hole.

A bird house to BRIGHTEN YOUR HOUSE!

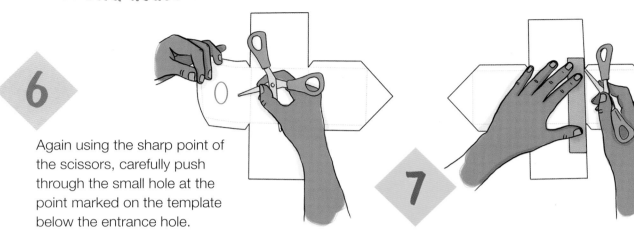

6

Again using the sharp point of the scissors, carefully push through the small hole at the point marked on the template below the entrance hole.

7

Now use the point of the scissors and a ruler to score gently along all the dotted lines on the template. Be careful not to press too hard or you will cut through the card.

8 Crease along all the score lines to make the box shape. Glue along the flaps and stick the bird house together.

9 To make the perch, take a strip of colored paper about 1¼ in (3 cm) wide and roll it up tightly until it fits snugly inside the smaller hole you made in the bird box.

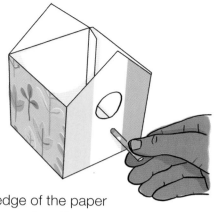

10 Glue down the edge of the paper to stop it from unraveling. Push the perch into the small hole.

11 Roughly cut out one bird template and stick it to the back of the paper you have chosen for your bird. Have the eye and perch hole position facing up, so that you can still see them. Cut the bird out carefully.

12 Use a hole punch to punch holes for the eye and perch in the positions marked. (Tip: if you are using a two-hole punch, practice first on some scrap paper so that you know exactly where the hole punch makes its hole—it's not always easy to tell!) Slide the bird onto the perch.

13 Roughly cut out one of the roof templates and stick it to the back of the colored paper you have chosen for the roof, with the score line upward so that you can still see it. Cut around the roof carefully. Using the point of the scissors and a ruler, lightly score across the score line. Crease along the score line and bend into the roof shape. Place the roof on the bird box.

Paper bells

These paper bell decorations are made by sticking eight bell shapes together. They look great in pretty pastel designs, but equally good in silver and gold when Christmas comes.

You will need

Plain paper or thin card for template

Scissors

A pencil

Eight 8½ x 11-in (210 x 297-mm/A4) sheets of wrapping paper per bell

A glue stick

Ribbon

Beads

Strong thread

Sticky tape

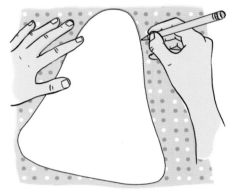

1 Ask an adult to help you photocopy the bell template on page 121. If you can copy straight onto thin card, it will make the template stronger and easier to use. Cut out the bell shape. Place the template on the back of the wrapping paper and draw around it, using a pencil.

2 Carefully cut out the bell shape. In total, you will need eight bell shapes in different-colored papers for one finished bell. It's easier to cut out all the shapes in one go.

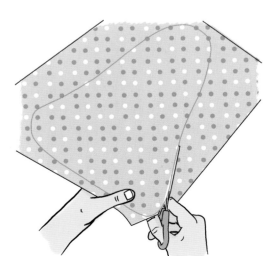

3 Fold each bell in half lengthwise, making sure that the pretty pattern is on the inside.

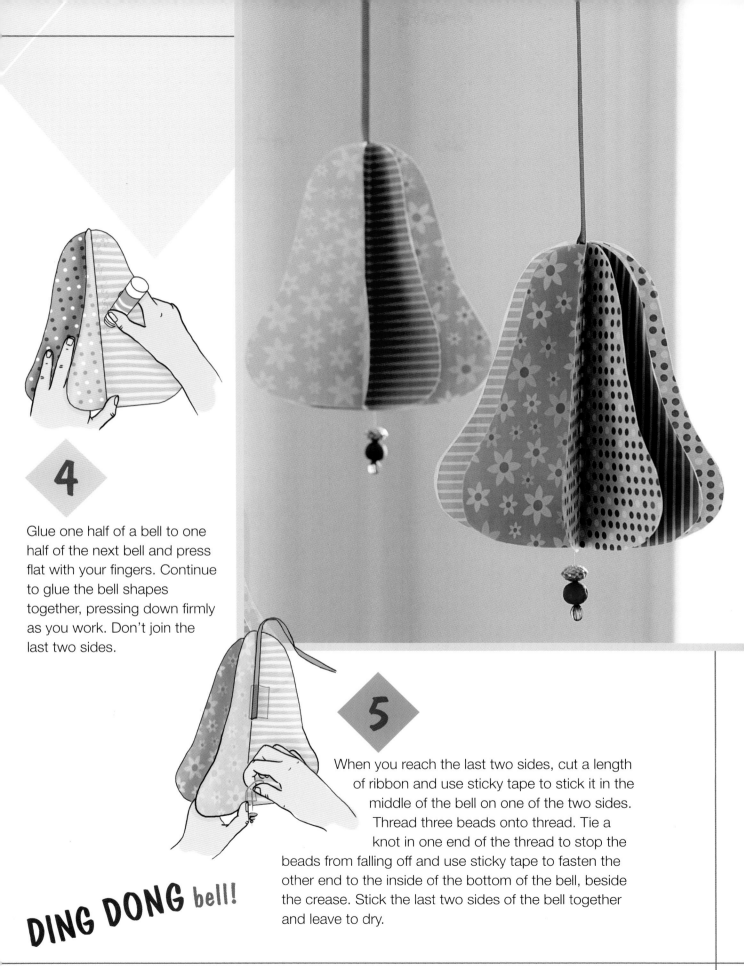

4

Glue one half of a bell to one half of the next bell and press flat with your fingers. Continue to glue the bell shapes together, pressing down firmly as you work. Don't join the last two sides.

5

When you reach the last two sides, cut a length of ribbon and use sticky tape to stick it in the middle of the bell on one of the two sides. Thread three beads onto thread. Tie a knot in one end of the thread to stop the beads from falling off and use sticky tape to fasten the other end to the inside of the bottom of the bell, beside the crease. Stick the last two sides of the bell together and leave to dry.

DING DONG bell!

Chinese lanterns

Paper lanterns are traditional, simple, and make very pretty Christmas decorations. These ones are made from soft pink and silver wrappings and have a trimming of sequins for an extra special touch, but you could make them in any size or color and decorate them with stars, stickers, or shiny ribbon.

You will need

Pretty wrapping paper

Scissors

A pencil

A ruler

A glue stick

8 in (20 cm) sequin trim per lantern (or shiny ribbon or stickers)

1 Cut a square of paper measuring 8 x 8 in (20 x 20 cm) for the lantern and a strip of paper ¾ x 8 in (2 x 20 cm) for the handle. Fold the square of paper in half and press flat.

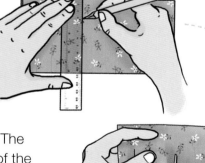

2 Take the piece of folded paper and, cutting inward from the folded edge of the paper, cut slits that finish about 1¼ in (3 cm) from the top of the paper. The first one should be about ¾ in (2 cm) from the edge of the paper, the next one ¾ in (2 cm) from the first—and so on until you reach the other edge. You may want to mark the lines using a pencil and a ruler first, to make it easier to cut the paper neatly.

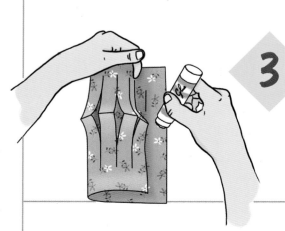

3 To make the lantern, unfold the paper and roll it to form a tube, with the paper slits running from top to bottom. Glue the edges of the paper together. When the glue is dry, press downward gently so that the cut paper splays outward into a lantern shape.

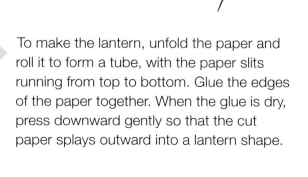

4

To finish, cut a piece of sequin trim to fit around the top of the lantern and glue it in place. Glue the ends of the hanging loop to the inside of the lantern on both sides and let the glue dry completely.

Hang up your lantern where the sequins will catch the light and sparkle!

PRETTY LANTERNS to decorate your home!

Christmas crackers

Making your own crackers is fun, and you can fill them with cool presents and your favorite silly jokes. Make the crackers from colorful wrapping paper, and trim them with sequins or glitter to make your Christmas dinner table really sparkle.

You will need

Cardboard toilet rolls

8 x 12 in (20 x 30 cm) piece of paper per cracker

A pencil

A ruler

Scissors

Sticky tape

A glue stick

Snaps for crackers (you can buy them from craft shops or online)

Gifts, paper hats, and jokes

8 in (20 cm) ribbon, ¼ in (5 mm) wide, per cracker

Sequin trim

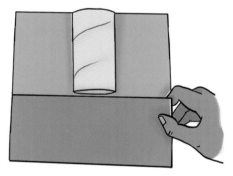

1 Lay the paper flat on the table, colored side facing down. Put one end of the toilet roll in the middle, just touching one end of the paper, and fold the other end of the paper so that it just meets the toilet roll. Unfold it to leave a crease.

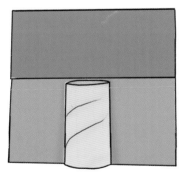

2 Move the toilet roll to the opposite end of the paper and do the same as you did in step 1. You will now have two creases across your paper and the toilet roll will fit between them exactly.

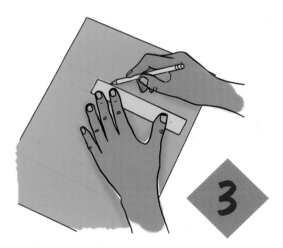

3 Measure 1 in (2.5 cm) out from the bottom crease and draw a line across the paper. Do the same for the top crease. Turn the paper over and fold back the paper along these lines.

4 At both ends, mark lines inward from the folded edge, ¾ in (2 cm) apart, starting about 1 in (2.5 cm) in from the outside edge of the paper. These lines should reach as far as the two creases you first made.

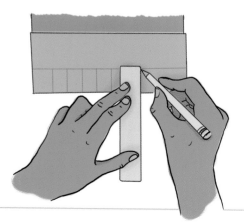

5 Cut from the fold along the lines to create slits in the paper. These slits make it easier to tie the cracker ends.

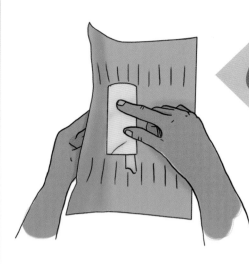

6 Now unfold the paper and lay it flat, colored side facing down. Place the cardboard roll on top. Use a small piece of sticky tape to hold the paper onto the roll. Now wrap the paper around the roll as tightly as you can.

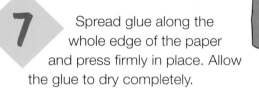

7 Spread glue along the whole edge of the paper and press firmly in place. Allow the glue to dry completely.

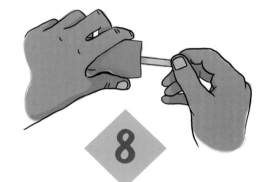

8 Push the cracker snap through the open end of the roll. This is also the time to fill the cracker with your gift, a joke, and, perhaps, a paper hat.

9 Gently tie a 4-in (10-cm) length of ribbon around one end of the cracker and tie it in a knot. Repeat at the other end.

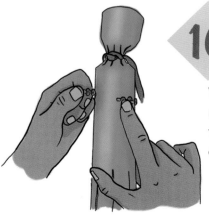

10 Wrap some sequin trim around the cracker to measure how much you need. Cut three pieces to this length. Glue the sequin trim in rows around the cracker. Allow the glue to dry completely.

Chopstick wrapper

Are you planning a party with Chinese food for Chinese New Year or is there another special occasion when you will be eating Asian food? You could make your table look very fine with these easy-to-make chopstick wrappers. Make one for each member of the party with the person's name on it. The ones in the photo are decorated with cherry blossom and maple leaves, but you could decorate yours with lions and dragons.

You will need

1 sheet of paper, 7 x 12 in (18 x 30 cm)

Paper shapes to decorate

A glue stick

A pen

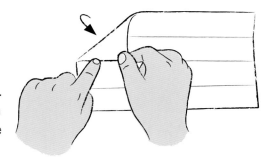

1 Fold the paper in half and open it out again. Fold the top and bottom in to the center and crease them. Open the paper out. You will have three creases. Lay the paper down with the creases going from side to side. Turn the top left corner down to the center crease.

2 Starting from the bottom, fold the paper up along the first crease, turn it over again along the middle crease, and then over again along the top crease.

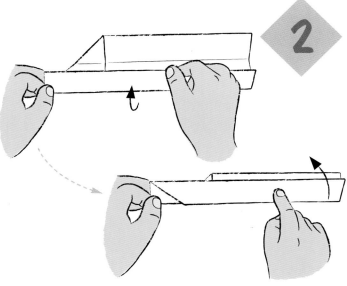

Chopstick holders for a very SPECIAL meal!

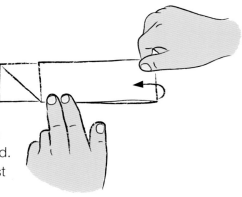

3 You now have a narrow strip with a diagonal fold at the left-hand end. Fold over the right hand end, so it just reaches the diagonal fold, and crease it.

4 Now take the same end and fold it up on a diagonal crease, so that it is at right angles to the other end of the strip.

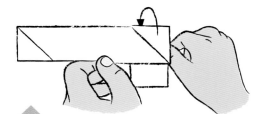

5 Lift the paper and wrap this same end once around the bottom of the chopstick holder.

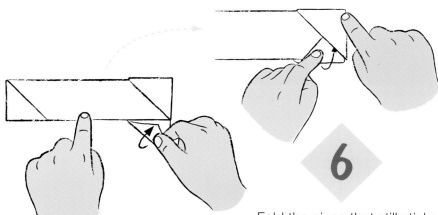

6 Fold the piece that still sticks out into a triangle along the side of the chopstick holder before turning it up and tucking it in place behind the fold.

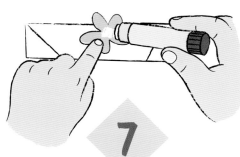

7

Cut out shapes to stick onto your chopstick holder or decorate it using a pen.

Slip the sharp end of your chopsticks inside the wrapper!

Paper flowers

Paper flowers are colorful and easy to make with colored card and tissue paper. You can give them pipe-cleaner stems and gather them into bouquets, or use them as jewelry or to decorate birthday cards.

You will need

Paper for flower template

A pencil

Scissors

Colored card

Colored tissue paper or crêpe paper

Glue stick

Sticky tape

Pipe cleaners (green is best)

1 Trace the flower template on page 120 onto paper and cut it out. Draw around the template on colored card and cut out the flower shape carefully.

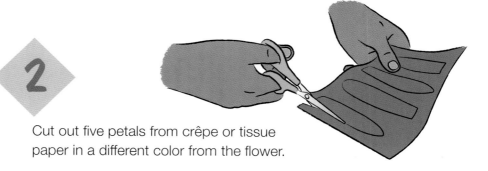

2 Cut out five petals from crêpe or tissue paper in a different color from the flower.

3 Fold a small pleat in the bottom end of each petal. Use the glue stick to glue the end of a petal to the center of the card flower. Repeat for each petal, then let the glue dry completely.

4 Find a small round object (about 1 in/2 cm across) and draw around it on colored card. Cut out this small circle and glue it to the center of the flower to cover the ends of the petals. Use a small piece of sticky tape to attach a pipe cleaner to the back of the flower to form a stem.

EASY-TO-MAKE, beautiful flowers!

CHAPTER FIVE

Gorgeous Gifts and Cards

Folded paper fan

For summer days and party fun, make this lovely fan and decorate it with flowers, ribbon, and glitter. Two long sticks to hold it together give it the professional touch. You will need a very long piece of paper for this—but if you haven't got one, try gluing smaller pieces together before you start.

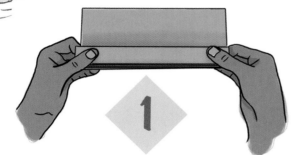

1

Place the piece of paper flat on the table in front of you. Starting at the end closest to you, fold up a strip about 1 in (2.5 cm) wide. Make a sharp crease. Turn the paper over. Fold up the fold you have just made. Turn the paper back over again and repeat, turning up both folds. Try to make the folds all the same width. Keep going like this, making concertina folds, right to the end of the paper. Press each fold really flat.

2

If you want, you can leave the concertina paper under a heavy book overnight to make it as flat as possible.

3

Open out the paper to its full length again and use the marker pen to draw flowers all over it at evenly-spaced intervals. Spread some glue on the centers of about five or six of the flowers and sprinkle on the glitter. Shake off any excess glitter onto a piece of scrap paper and then pour it back into the pot to reuse on other flowers.

A glittery fan for hot **SUMMER DAYS!**

4

Repeat until all the flower
centers are covered in
glitter. Allow the glue to
dry completely.

5

Hold the two wooden battens
together with a couple of elastic
bands at one end. Spread glue down
8 in (20 cm) of the other end of one batten
and attach one end of the pleated paper to
it. Leave to dry.

6

When the first side is
dry, keeping the fan flat
on the table, bring the
other side around in a
circle and glue that to the
other batten. Leave the
glue to dry. Remove the
elastic bands. Now glue
three lengths of ribbon to
the top of each stick for
a finishing touch.

Easter basket

Will you be having an Easter Egg hunt this Easter? If you are, you could make an Easter basket, like this one, for yourself and each of the other hunters to collect your eggs in. Decorate each basket in pretty pastel colors. Cut out chicks and Easter bunnies from wrapping paper, and stick them on. Use rubber stamps to make pretty borders and strips of ribbon for a sophisticated touch.

COLLECT EGGS in this Easter basket!

You will need

----

11 x 17 in (297 x 240 mm/ A3) photocopy card in pastel colors

A ruler and pencil

Double-sided sticky tape

A glue stick

Scissors

A hole punch

¼-in (6-mm) ribbon in pastel colors (optional)

Easter-themed wrapping paper

Rubber flower stamps (optional)

Brass paper fasteners

1 Ask an adult to photocopy the template on page 126 onto colored card, using the 200% zoom on the photocopier. Cut the basket out. Cut along all the solid lines, making sure that you cut down the sides right to the corners of the center square. Do not cut along the dotted lines.

2 Using the point of a pair of scissors and a ruler, carefully score along all of the dotted lines. Fold your basket into shape, neatly folding in each of the flaps. Then flatten it out again.

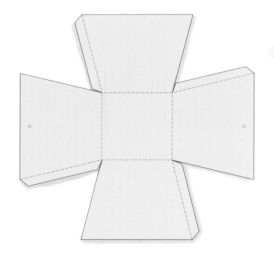

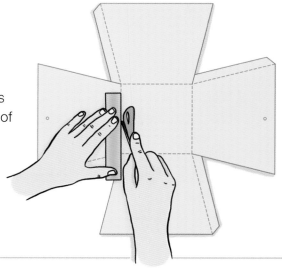

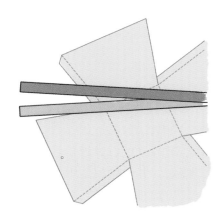

3

For the handle, cut two strips of colored card, each ½ x 9 in (1.5 x 23 cm). These look pretty in two different colors.

4

Use a hole punch to punch a hole in the two places marked on the template. (Tip: this is easy with a single-hole punch; if you only have a double one, experiment on scrap paper first to find exactly where the punch makes the hole). These holes are for attaching the handle. Lay the two handle pieces on top of each other and punch a hole at both ends. Put the handle pieces to one side.

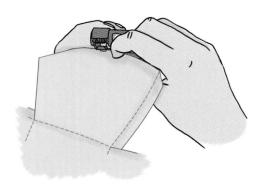

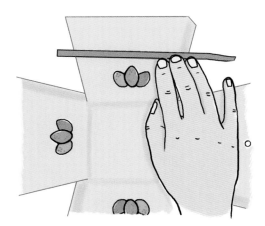

5

Turn the card over so that the dotted lines don't show. Decorate each side of your basket. Remember that the square is the bottom of your basket—be sure that any pictures are the right way up! Use thin strips of double-sided tape to attach the ribbon to avoid a gluey mess.

6

Now put a strip of double-sided sticky tape along each of the flaps (on the outside, next to the decorations).

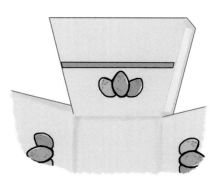

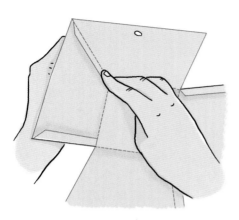

7 Turn the card over, fold up the sides and, one by one, remove the backing from the sticky tape strips and fasten the sides together.

8 Use paper fasteners through the punched holes to attach the handle to the inside of the basket.

Fill the basket with eggs as an Easter present!

9 Line your basket with some straw or crumpled tissue paper as a nest for your eggs.

Pop-up cards

Once you realize how these cards work, you can create all sorts of pop-up surprises for Christmas, birthdays, Easter, and other celebrations. The trick lies in leaving two points of the pop-up attached to the outside of the card, while the rest is cut free.

You will need

Plain green card

Scissors

A pencil

Paper

Paints

A paintbrush

A rubber

1 Take a rectangle of card about 8¼ x 11¾ in (210 x 297 mm/A4 size) and fold it in half. Trace the Christmas tree template on page 122 onto a piece of paper and cut it out. Place the template on the folded card, with the flat edge against the fold of the card, and draw around it. Mark on the dotted line at the widest point of the tree.

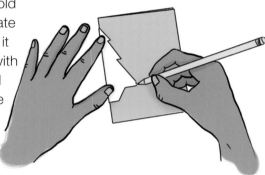

2 Carefully cut around the outline of the tree through both layers of the card. Be sure not to cut through the section you have marked with a dotted line at the widest point of the tree. These two sections (one on each side) keep the pop-up tree attached to the card itself. When you have finished, rub out the dotted line.

3 Open out the card and gently push the Christmas tree shape forward so that it stands away from the folded card to create a 3-D effect. Now you can see how important the un-cut side sections are, because they keep the tree shape attached to the card.

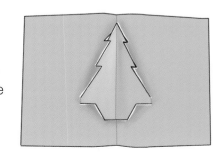

4 Use a fine paintbrush to draw decorations on the tree. Add small gift boxes scattered around the tree and some glitter for sparkle.

A card with a pop-up SURPRISE!

Rosette card

These stunning 3-D cards are very simple to make. You could choose matching colors like the ones shown—red papers on a red background—or go wild with your choice of different colors and patterns. Make big cards with several rosettes and gift tags with one tiny one.

You will need

Pieces of patterned paper

A pencil

A ruler

Scissors

A stapler

A glue stick

Cream card

Plain colored paper

PVA glue

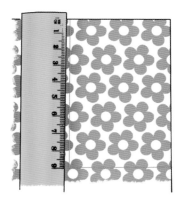

1 Cut out three or four rectangles of patterned paper measuring 2½ x 3½ in (6 x 9 cm).

2 Take one rectangle of paper and lay it on the table with a short side toward you. Fold up a strip of about ¼ in (7 mm) and make a sharp crease. Turn the paper over. Fold up the fold you have just made. Turn the paper back over again and repeat, turning up both folds. Try to make the folds all the same width. Keep going like this to the end of the paper to make a concertina.

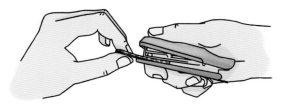

3 Fold your concertina paper in half to find the exact center, then staple the paper together horizontally across the center point.

4 Cut the ends into a rounded shape.

5

Open out the rosette and glue the edges together to form a complete circle. Hold the glued edges tightly in place until dry. Make two or three more rosettes in this way.

6

Cut a 7½ x 5-in (19 x 13-cm) rectangle of plain colored paper and a 5½ x 16-in (14 x 40.5-cm) rectangle of cream card. Fold the card in half widthwise. Glue the plain paper rectangle onto the front of the cream card with glue stick.

7

Arrange the rosettes on the card and then glue them on with small dabs of PVA glue.

Russian doll card

Real Russian dolls nest inside each other: open one doll and you will find a smaller one inside it. This folding card looks like those dolls and you can decorate it as brightly as you want, making each doll a different color and pattern. You will have to ask an adult to help you with some photocopying first.

You will need

A pencil

Adhesive putty (Blu Tack)

12 x 5 in (30 x 12.5 cm) thin white card

Scissors

Scraps of different patterned papers

Scraps of plain bright colored paper for the heads

A glue stick

A fine felt-tip pen

A ruler

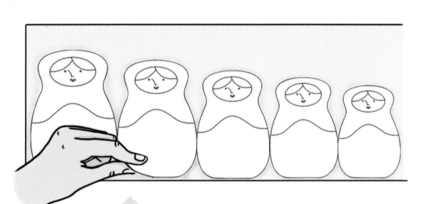

1 Ask an adult to photocopy the doll template five times, starting at full size and then reducing the size by 8% each time. Cut out the five templates. Using small pieces of adhesive putty, stick each of the doll templates, in order of size, onto the white card. Make sure that the bottom of each doll touches the bottom of the card and that the sides of the dolls are touching.

2 Draw around the row of dolls. Take off the templates and put them to one side. Cut out the whole row of dolls, keeping them joined together.

Five Russian dolls, all **IN A ROW!**

3

Take the biggest template. Choose a pattern of paper to decorate this doll, then draw round the template onto the paper. Cut out the shape and stick it to the matching cardboard doll. Do the same for each of the other dolls.

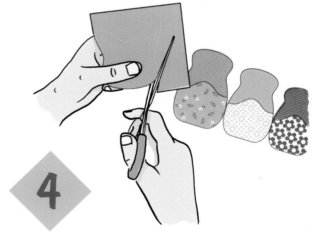

4

Next take the biggest template again and cut the head part off the body part. Draw around the head part onto brightly colored plain paper. Cut out the shape and stick it on top of the matching doll. Do the same for each of the other dolls.

5 Now cut out the five faces from the templates. Color in the hair and draw over the mouth in red.

6 Stick each face onto the matching body.

7 Finally, turn the card over and, using the point of the scissors and a ruler, score down where each doll joins the next. Fold the dolls back and forward to make a concertina shape that will stand up.

Candy bags

At the end of a party, why not give your guests treats of candy wrapped in these lovely little bags? Use pastel colors for pastel sweets and bold colors for brighter sweets.

You will need

1 sheet of 8½ x 11-in (210 x 297-mm/A4) card

Sheets of 8½ x 11-in (210 x 297-mm/A4) paper

A pencil

A ruler

Scissors with pointed tips

Double-sided sticky tape

Small candies to fill the bags

GUESS what's in the CANDY bag!

1 Cut out a rectangle of card measuring 5 x 6¾ in (12.5 x 17 cm). Use this as a template to cut out rectangles of colored paper, one for each guest.

2 Take the first rectangle of paper. Cut a thin strip of double-sided sticky tape, 5 in (12.5 cm) long and about ¼ in (6 mm) wide, and stick this along one of the 5-in (12.5-cm) edges, on the wrong side of the paper.

3 Remove the backing paper from the tape. Line up the two opposite edges and stick them together, but don't flatten the curved pouch shape.

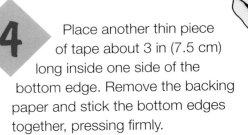

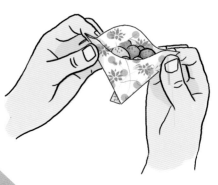

4 Place another thin piece of tape about 3 in (7.5 cm) long inside one side of the bottom edge. Remove the backing paper and stick the bottom edges together, pressing firmly.

5 Place a few candies in the pouch. If you're using homemade candies, wrap them in plastic first, so that the grease doesn't stain the paper.

6 Flatten down the open end of the tube in the opposite direction to the closed end, so that the side join is right in the middle. This makes the pyramid shape. Press flat at each side edge with your fingers and thumbs to mark where to place the tape. Place a thin strip of tape about 3 in (7.5 cm) along the inside of the opening, lining up the ends with the creases you made in step 4. Remove the tape backing and stick down the edges.

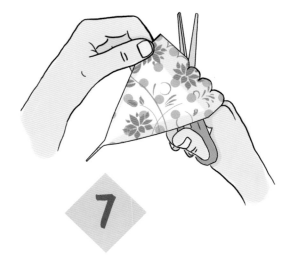

7 Using a pencil, draw a line of scallops along both top and bottom seams. Cut out the scallop edging along both edges, using a small pair of scissors with pointed tips.

Tiny gift box

This traditional origami design is perfect for holding little treats. You could make one for each of your friends to take home after a birthday party instead of a party bag. You can make them in any size. Small ones are quite fiddly, so use bigger paper when you first make one.

You will need

1 square sheet of paper (a pretty design will make for a colorful box)

1 Fold the piece of paper in half, then open it out. Turn the paper through 90° and fold it in half again. Open out the paper. You will have two folds, which make a cross on your paper.

2 Fold all four corners in to the center.

3 Fold the paper back on itself with flat sides together and then fold it in half from right to left.

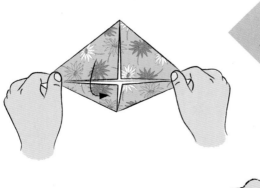

4 Stand the top triangle upright, put your fingers between the two layers, and pull them apart. The pocket will open out and you can flatten it down to make a diamond shape.

Beautiful boxes to fill with **TINY TREATS!**

5 Turn the paper over and repeat the previous step: stand the large triangle up, put your fingers between the two layers, and pull them apart. Flatten them down into a diamond shape on top of the other one.

6 Place your fingers inside the slit in the diamond shape as far as they will go. Pull the flaps out and fold the paper down toward you into a rectangle.

7 Turn the paper over and repeat step 6 on the other side, folding it into a rectangle so that the paper is left in the shape of a simple house.

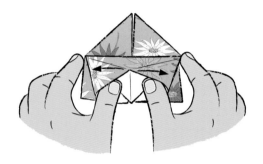

8 Turn over one of the side flaps on the front of the candy box, so that the house shape has no folds—just a slit down the middle. Turn it over and do the same on the back.

9 Lift the top flaps on both the left and the right and fold them in half, so that they meet in the center.

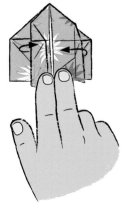

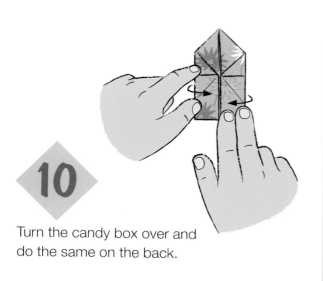

10

Turn the candy box over and do the same on the back.

11

Fold the top triangle forward over the box on the front and then on the back.

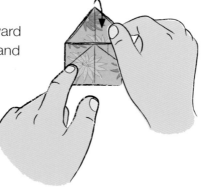

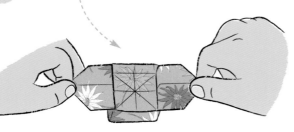

12

Gently open out the candy box, flattening the bottom of the box and pulling the pointed flaps apart. When complete, the base of the little box is raised off the ground—the sides do not bend under.

Hide tiny treasures inside your box!

Basic techniques

Origami is very simple. All you need to make wonderful models is a steady hand and some patience. There are some folds that are trickier than others and the easiest way to learn them is to ask someone to show you, but these instructions will help you to master the basic techniques.

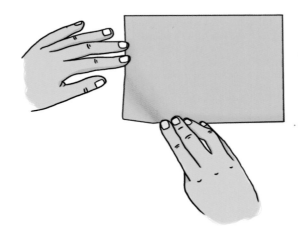

Making folds

Origami is all about folding! Learning how to make crisp, even folds will lead to wonderful paper creations.

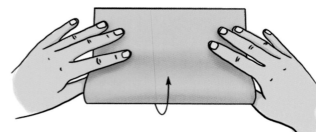

1 When you make a fold, make sure that the paper lies exactly where you want it, with the corners sitting exactly on top of each other.

2 As you make the crease, make sure that you keep the paper completely still so that the fold is perfectly true and straight.

3 Still holding the paper with your spare hand, use a ruler or the side of a pencil to press down the fold until it is as flat as possible.

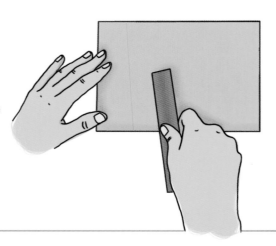

Opening folds

Sometimes you will need to open out a crease and refold the paper so that it lies in a new shape, as in the triangle fold shown here.

1 Lift the flap to be opened and begin pulling the two sides apart.

2 As the space widens, you will need to make sure that the point folds properly—so use a pencil to gently pull the paper open.

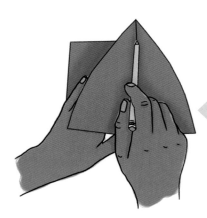

3 As the two corners separate, the top point drops forward and the square flattens out into a triangle.

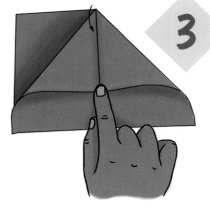

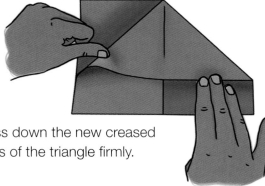

4 Press down the new creased sides of the triangle firmly.

Inside folds

These are probably the trickiest folds to do and need a bit of practice.

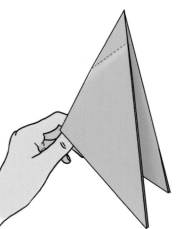

1 Following the dotted line in the diagram, make a crease at the tip of the triangle.

2 Now unfold it and fold it back the other way along the same crease.

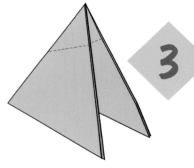

3 Open out the paper again.

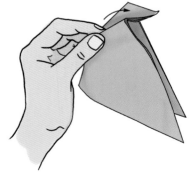

4 Push the top crease down between the two other creases to make a "valley" fold.

5 Smooth the top creases so that the "valley" is tucked inside.

Key to arrows

Throughout this book, you'll see that the artworks include arrows to show you what to do. Here's what they all mean:

Fold
Fold the part of the paper shown in this direction.

Folding direction
Fold the whole paper over in this direction.

Open out
Open out and refold the paper over in the direction shown.

Change the position
Spin the paper 90° (one right angle) in the direction of the arrows.

Change the position
Spin the paper through 180° (two right angles —top goes to bottom or right goes to left).

Turn over
Turn the paper over.

Make a crease
Fold the paper over in the direction of the arrow, then open it out again.

Templates

This section contains all the templates you will need for the projects. The templates on pages 120—122 are full size, so to use them you just have to trace them off the page. You don't have to use the template on page 123 for the millefeuille cake, but it acts as a helpful guide if you want to color in your own paper to make it. The templates on pages 124—126 are all half-size templates—this means that you need to ask an adult to help you photocopy the templates, using the 200% zoom button on the photocopier.

PAPER FLOWERS

PAGE 92

PAPER BELLS

PAGE 82

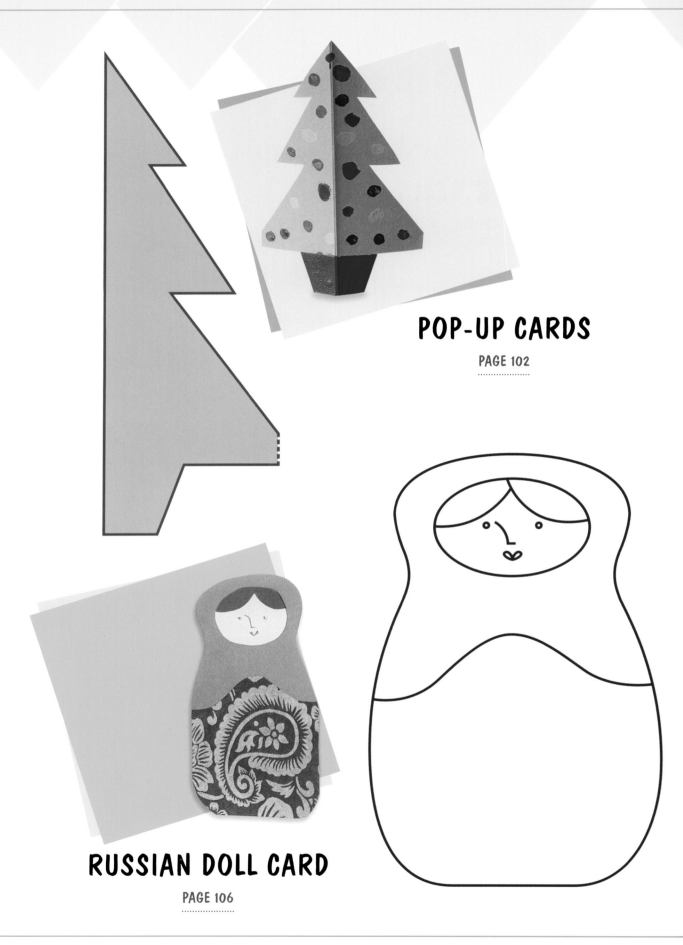

POP-UP CARDS

PAGE 102

RUSSIAN DOLL CARD

PAGE 106

MILLEFEUILLE CAKE

PAGE 68

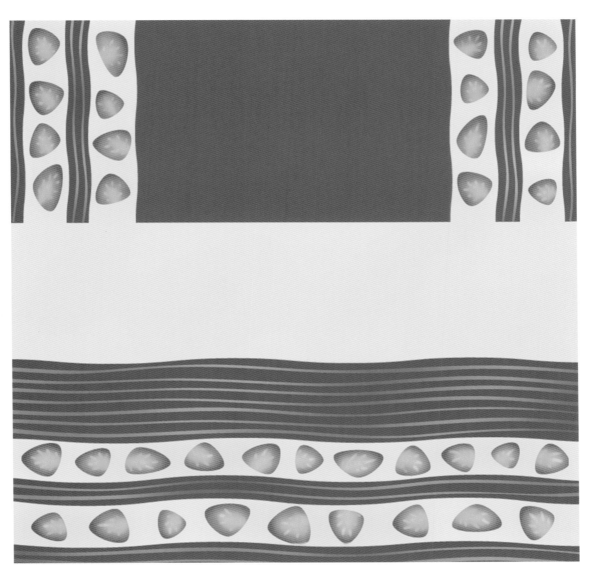

BIRD BOXES

PAGE 78

The templates on these pages are all half-size templates—this means you need to ask an adult to help you photocopy the templates, using the 200% zoom button on the photocopier.

Roof of bird house

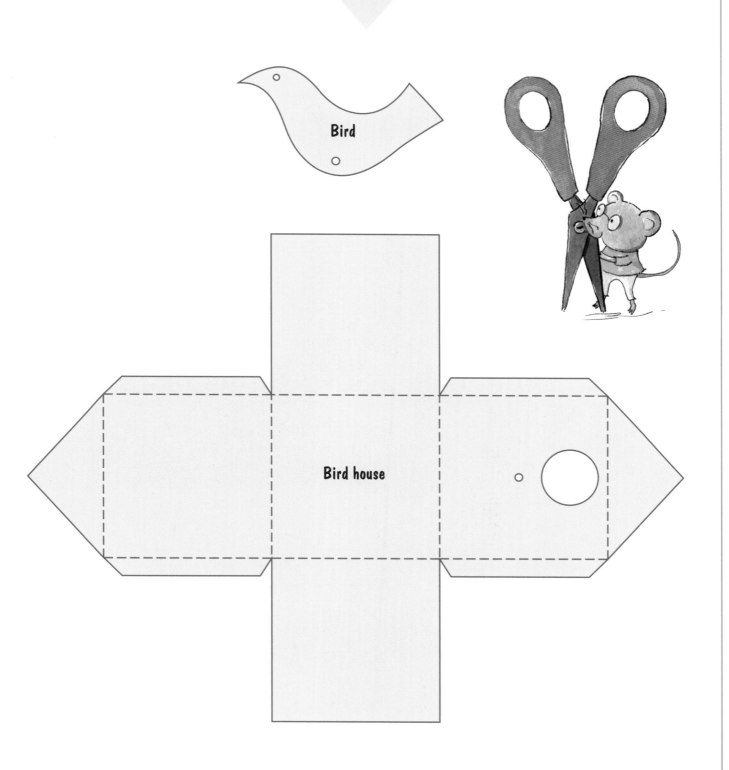

Bird

Bird house

EASTER BASKET

PAGE 98

The template on this page is a half-size template—this means you need to ask an adult to help you photocopy it, using the 200% zoom button on the photocopier.

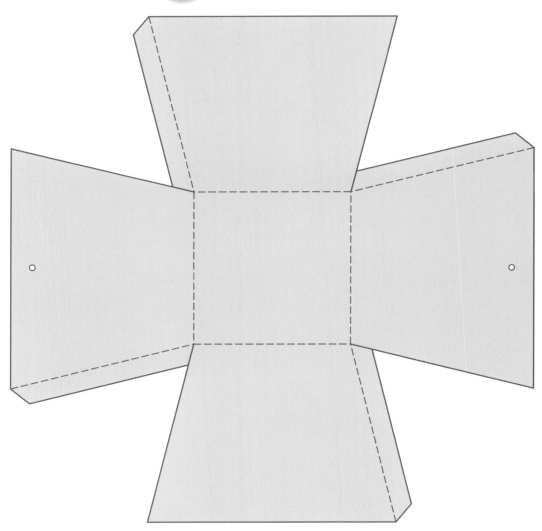

Suppliers

Origami paper is available at most good paper stores or online. Here are a few sources, as well as stores with general papercrafting supplies.

USA

A C Moore
www.acmoore.com

Dick Blick Art Materials
www.dickblick.com

Hobby Lobby
www.hobbylobby.com

JPT America, Inc
www.jptamerica.com

Jo-Ann Fabric and Craft Store
www.joann.com

Michaels Stores
www.michaels.com

Origami Stores and Suppliers
www.origamisources.com

Paper Source
www.paper-source.com

UK

B&Q (for wooden battens)
www.diy.com

Calico Crafts
www.calicocrafts.co.uk

Creations Art and Craft Materials
www.ecreations.co.uk

Hobbycraft
www.hobbycraft.co.uk

JP-Books
www.jpbooks.co.uk/en

Japan Centre
www.japancentre.com

The Japanese Shop (online only)
www.thejapaneseshop.co.uk

London Graphic Centre
www.londongraphics.co.uk

Paperchase
www.paperchase.co.uk

Acknowledgments

Key: l = left, r = right, t = top, b = bottom, c = center

Project makers

Mari Ono and Roshin Ono: 10–11, 16–29, 32–47, 55–73, 112–115

Mari Ono: 50–54, 89–91

Emma Hardy: 104–105

Catherine Woram: 12–15, 82–88, 92–93, 96–97, 102–103

Clare Youngs: 76–81, 106–111

Fiona Jones: 98–101

Photography

Carolyn Barber: 1, 4, 6b, 8, 9t, 16–29, 32–33, 55–73, 95b, 112–115, 123

Geoff Dann: 2, 5b, 10–11, 30–31, 34–49, 50–54, 89–91

Claire Richardson: 75t, 76–81, 94, 106–111, 122b, 124

Tino Tedaldi: 5t, 95t, 98–101, 104-105, 125

Polly Wreford: 3, 6t, 7, 9b, 12–15, 74, 82–88, 96–97, 102–103, 121, 122t

Vanessa Davies: 75b, 92–93, 120

Jacket photography

Back cover: Carolyn Barber (tl), Claire Richardson (r), Polly Wreford (bl); spine: Polly Wreford; front cover: Carolyn Barber, Polly Wreford (bl), Tino Tedaldi (bc), Geoff Dann (br)

Styling

Trina Dalziel: 2, 10–11, 30, 34–47

Rose Hammick: 4, 8, 16–29, 32–33, 48, 55–73, 112–115

Georgina Harris: 5t, 50–54, 89–91, 104–105

Catherine Woram: 3, 7, 12–15, 74, 82–88, 92–93, 96–97, 102–103

Index

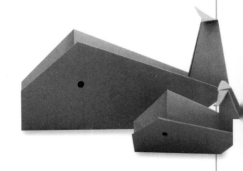